WAR IN THE PACIFIC

The most important, explosive, and strategic battles of World War Two took place in the Pacific arena, as the seemingly invincible Japanese sought to expand their notorious empire. Now this astonishing era comes to life in a breathtakingly authentic new series by noted historian Edwin P. Hoyt that places the reader in the heart of the earth-shattering conflict—a dramatic, detailed chronicle of military brilliance and extraordinary human courage on the bloody battlefields of land and sea.

VOLUME
V

ALEUTIANS

WAR IN THE PACIFIC

VOLUME V

ALEUTIANS

EDWIN P. HOYT

AVON BOOKS ◆ NEW YORK

WAR IN THE PACIFIC, VOLUME V: ALEUTIANS is an original publication of Avon Books. This work has never before appeared in book form.

AVON BOOKS
A division of
The Hearst Corporation
1350 Avenue of the Americas
New York, New York 10019

Copyright © 1992 by Edwin P. Hoyt
Published by arrangement with the author
Library of Congress Catalog Card Number: 91-92415
ISBN: 0-380-76316-8

First Avon Books Printing: May 1992

AVON TRADEMARK REG. U.S. PAT. OFF. AND IN OTHER COUNTRIES, MARCA REGISTRADA, HECHO EN U.S.A.

Printed in the U.S.A.

RA 10 9 8 7 6 5 4 3 2 1

CONTENTS

Preface   1

1. Preparing for War   9
2. Defense of Hawaii   14
3. The Western Perimeter   28
4. Against Sabotage and Espionage   46
5. West Coast Defense   50
6. The Decision   54
7. Striking the American Perimeter
   in the South   57
8. First Midway, Then Hawaii   61
9. Alaskan Defenses   73
10. When the Japanese Came   77
11. The Japanese Attack   82
12. Arctic War   89
13. Problems of Command   92
14. The Japanese Problem   102
15. Enter Admiral Kinkaid   106
16. Wearing Down the Enemy   112
17. The Battle of the Komandorski Islands   118
18. Attu   128
19. The Landings on Attu   134
20. On Attu   138
21. The Fight for Attu   142
22. The Fall of Attu   147
23. The Battle for Kiska   152
24. The Invasion of Kiska   160
25. Exit the Aleutians   167

Notes   170

Bibliography   175

Index   177

PREFACE

To understand what happened in the Aleutian Islands in World War II, and its effect on the people of the United States, one must go back to basic American principles and beliefs. The United States has long considered itself unique among nations, partly because of the geographical nature of the country, protected by two great oceans, and partly because of its historical lack of interest in colonial expansion until the last of the nineteenth century. When it did become a colonial power, the United States was always uncomfortable in that role, and it still is today.

Even in its adventures in Latin America, and they were many, the United States was always essentially guided by a paternal interest in preserving the Western Hemisphere from foreign—and particularly European—incursion. Following George Washington's warnings about the danger of entangling alliances, from James Monroe to Woodrow Wilson the nation was led by men with a Calvinistic sense of mission to bend the Americas into an American mold. This attitude and behavior were not always appreciated by America's neighbors, but in the years after World War I, a better accommodation between the United States and its neighbors began to appear.

The possibility of a serious attack from any source appeared remote in the early 1900s, and even until the late 1930s attack by land-based air power was virtually impossible. In those days, too, the power of the aircraft carrier was only imperfectly understood. It took the beginning of World War II in Europe and particularly the British carrier plane strike on the Italian fleet at Taranto to make the world conscious that air power had come so completely of age that no place in the world could be considered totally safe from attack.

In the years after World War I, air power was suspect by both army and navy. The army had concentrated its efforts on protecting the continental United States against attack from the sea. This attitude of defense also applied to the Panama Canal Zone, the Hawaiian Islands, and Alaska and its outlying islands.

With the rise of the Italian and German dictatorships, American military men and diplomats began thinking in terms of hemispheric defense. As Adolf Hitler gave evidence that he was going to plunge the Western world into war, American leaders began to feel the need to forestall the establishment of any hostile air base or other military base in the Western Hemisphere from which the United States, its possessions, and the Panama Canal could be attacked.

From the date of the Munich appeasement of Hitler in 1938, this American attitude began to become policy. Hemispheric defense became the essence of U. S. military policy and remained so. Virtually everything the United States did in foreign affairs was aimed at protecting itself from attack. To do this, the United States had to protect its neighbors as well, particularly the weaker ones, which might be subject to pressures. At first all eyes were on Europe. Early on Italy was seen as a potential aggressor, but Benito Mussolini was soon eclipsed by Hitler. When the Japanese began their serious efforts to force China into their own mold, President Franklin D. Roosevelt and Secretary of State Cordell Hull added Japan definitely to the list of potential aggressive enemies. Japan had long been a candidate for the list, particularly since its manipulations in Manchuria and North China, which had begun in 1928. Looking ahead at an unsettled world increasingly dominated by totalitarians, American leaders could see the danger of Germany dominating Europe; Japan dominating the Eastern Hemisphere; and the two combining with Italy to dominate Africa, to wreck the British Empire, and eventually to threaten the Western Hemisphere with conquest. These fears in 1938 were very real and were later illustrated by the 1940 Rome-Berlin-Tokyo alliance that was so obviously directed against the United States that no one could miss its implications.

As for Japan, the seriousness of its intentions in China were unmistakable after 1937, and from that time on, dating from the incident in the battle for Nanking in which the American gunboat *Panay* was sunk deliberately by Japanese airmen, the threat of war with Japan was constant and growing. The military was concerned with the possibility that Japan might approach attack on the United States by first securing bases in the Aleutian Islands and Hawaii, or Midway and Wake islands. In view of its nearness to Japanese-mandated territory under the League of Nations, Guam, in the Marianas group, had to be written off from the first as an indefensible outpost, but not so Wake, Midway, Hawaii, and the Aleutians. The possibility that Japan might launch raids by aircraft carriers on American territory was definitely considered, particularly after Taranto. Even so, American military leaders believed the Japanese threat was secondary to the German threat. This attitude was largely historical in nature, dating back to the settling of America by Europeans and the relationship between powerful factions in the United States and Britain that was closer than the relationship between the United States and any other nations. Particularly after the European war began in 1939, America's military leaders saw the great danger to the United States and the Western Hemisphere in the possible defeat of Britain and France. The American military was well-aware of the widespread German influence in Latin America that had existed since before World War I and that had enabled the Germans in that war to maintain surface raiders in the Western Hemisphere for many months. As World War II developed the Germans became more open and voluble in Argentina, Uruguay, and Chile. This was a serious cause of concern in Washington.

This backdrop, as well as the German sinking of American merchant vessels on the high seas and the constant reminder of the German threat to the British lifeline to Canada and the United States, exacerbated the American concern for German aggression, quite overpowering the serious questions about the adventures of Japan. These became linked beyond doubt in 1940 when the Germans overran France and the Japanese took advantage of the French surrender to their German ally to force Vichy France to permit their occupation of northern Indochina. This Japanese step was taken to prepare for their conquest of Malaya, although their propaganda of the moment emphasized that their concern was only to "bring the China Incident to a successful and peaceful conclusion."

In 1940 American concern over the growing strength and success of Germany in its campaign of conquest persuaded American leaders that they must formalize the defense of the hemisphere. The situation with Canada was quite different. As a member of the British Commonwealth of Nations, Canada had gone to war with Germany when Britain went to war. Canadian troops were fighting in Europe, and Canadian vessels were braving the U-boat scourge to deliver supplies to Britain. In 1940 the United States and Canada formed a Permanent Joint Board on Defense, and in 1941 the two nations established a joint war plan.

The betterment of relations with America's southern neighbors, however, was a little more difficult to secure because of the long history of American intervention in Latin American affairs. Mexico, Central America, and South America had many reservations and even suspicions about America's intentions. Breaking these down was not an easy task, but by 1938 the announced Good Neighbor Policy and the American declaration that it would not intervene in Latin American affairs for any purpose had good results.

The Monroe Doctrine had proclaimed that Old World countries must not obtain control over any territory in the Western Hemisphere, either by force or by negotiation. Enforcing this policy had never previously been a real problem, but the German victories in Western Europe in 1940 gave it immediacy. Suddenly Germany had overrun the Netherlands, Denmark, and France, all of which had possessions in the New World. Germany also threatened to invade England momentarily. So suddenly the United States was confronted with a stark new problem: what to do about Vichy France and the German-dominated government of the

Netherlands and Denmark. The United States declared positively that no defense measures could be taken in the Western Hemisphere by these governments; the United States would assume full responsibility for their defense. Also, when the United States negotiated the arrangement by which it gave Britain fifty World War I vintage destroyers in exchange for the right to build and maintain bases in British possessions in the Western Hemisphere, the United States assumed the responsibility for the defense of these areas. As for Latin America, in 1940 the United States negotiated military agreements binding the United States to use its military forces to repel any attempted aggression in the Western Hemisphere.

By the middle of 1941 the American defense perimeter included Greenland, Newfoundland, Bermuda, Panama, and Puerto Rico on the Atlantic frontier, and Alaska, the Canal Zone, and Hawaii in the Pacific. That was the army plan. The navy also included Midway and Wake islands. Guam and Western Samoa were considered to remote to be included.

The movement of the United States fleet to Hawaii in 1941 was symbolic of the American intention to defend this perimeter, and was a warning to Japan. No such preparation needed to be made in the Atlantic region as long as the British Royal Navy continued to be strong. The German threat against the United States was seen realistically as coming from the sea and from German domination of the Old World powers who had Western Hemisphere possessions, while the Japanese threat, although perceived as less immediate, was also more direct. However, in 1940 the danger to Britain was such that the United States could not count on the permanent nature of the British naval dominance, and so plans had to be made for an enormous buildup of the American navy to be prepared to undertake sole hemispheric defense. That year the threat that worried American leaders most was that Britain would fall and the Germans would launch an assault on the United States from the northeast by way of Newfoundland and the St. Lawrence estuary. The American-Canadian Permanent Joint Board on Defense discussed this matter, and the American army prepared a plan to send an expeditionary force to repel such an invasion. President Roosevelt in 1940 then became interested in acquiring American military bases in Nova Scotia and Newfoundland.

In the spring of 1940, assessing the German threat as greater than the Japanese threat, President Roosevelt decided that all efforts should be made to avoid war with Japan so that defense could be concentrated against the German danger. The major concerns were the Caribbean and the Gulf of Mexico—the approaches to the Panama Canal. Two primary defense materials, oil and bauxite, came from these areas. As of June 1940 the presence of French colonies loyal to Vichy France complicated the problem. On the Atlantic side the point of concern was Brazil, which was largely undefended and not accessible for defense by American forces in the Caribbean. Therefore the U.S. government arranged with Pan American airways to construct two chains of airfields leading from the United States to eastern Brazil. The army was willing to operate these airfields, but the Brazilians would not agree to the stationing of any American forces in their country.

As the fall of France became imminent in May 1940, the American army prepared its hemispheric defense plan, Rainbow Four, which called for an American expeditionary force to be prepared to move to any threatened area. It looked good on paper, but at that time the American military forces were incapable of such action. The threat to Britain and the fear that it would not survive through 1940 was the compelling force in the American defensive attitude. The President and army and navy leaders decided that they were in no position to go to war with Japan or to intervene in Europe and must concentrate on the "South American situation," as President Roosevelt termed it. So Rainbow Four was the crystallization of the need to concentrate resources to ensure hemispheric defense.

The destroyers-for-bases exchange made with Britain in September 1940 presupposed that Britain could hold out for another six months. If Britain fell, the Germans in perhaps a year would be able to use the British fleet to launch an assault on the United States and Canada. For that reason enormous efforts began to raise the American army to a force of one and a half million in the next year, and to build many more ships capable of defending the Atlantic shores. The navy concentrated on building cruisers for that purpose, although when the war against Japan came, military planners quickly realized that aircraft carriers were more needed, and most of the cruiser hulls were converted in mid-construction. This destroyers-for-bases exchange, which gave outright aid to Britain, was the first open breach of American neutrality in the Second World War.

In 1940 Washington decided to avoid war with Japan at all costs in order to save Britain. Thus in a matter of weeks, American policy changed drastically, and any resemblance of neutrality in the European war was in effect discarded. America's leaders foresaw then the entry of the United States into the European conflict, at the expense of letting Japan continue its aggressive action in the Pacific. For this reason, American defenses in Alaska and the Aleutians were given short shrift. The American government did not want to annoy Japan and give it cause for action.

One major factor in the American preoccupation with events across the Atlantic was the belief of Secretary of War Henry L. Stimson that Japan would not go to war with the United States. This belief was also shared by the navy high command and communicated to President Roosevelt, who was convinced by it because it fit with his own concerns about the communality of interest with Britain. Thus the United States alternately threatened and cajoled the Japanese, never going so far as to create an open breach. But the Japanese leaders were not beguiled, and they saw in such meetings as the British-American-Dutch conferences on Southeast Asian defense an open threat to their economic lifelines. When in 1940 the Americans responded to the Japanese occupation of Indochina by cutting off Japanese oil and other strategic materials, Washington could not have known that the reaction of the Japanese would be immediate and decisive. By that time the Japanese army was in effective control of the Japanese government, in the sense that no cabinet could survive without army acquiescence. At that point the Japanese army and navy began to prepare definitely for war. The only question was where they would turn to get their necessary raw materials. Would they turn north to get Siberian oil and minerals? Would they turn south to get the resources from Southeast Asia? The decision to turn south was the result of two ill-fated military adventures against the Soviet Union in which the Japanese lost many thousands of men and learned that they were not prepared to confront a powerful military machine. Yet even as the Japanese military prepared for war, factions in Japan still hoped for peace and the success of negotiations with the United States. Japan had no territorial ambitions concerning America; its real interests ended on the Asian continent and in the Dutch East Indies. Japan's concern with the United States was prompted by fear of American intervention, particularly by the Pacific Fleet, in Asian affairs.

That is why Admiral Kichisabura Nomura was sent to America in 1941 to conduct negotiations with the United States. Japan's hope was that the Americans would recognize its ambition in Asia to unite the Asian people under Japanese leadership and to eliminate European colonialism. The Japanese were ambivalent about America, but they never lost sight of the fact that the Americans had engaged to free their Philippine colony, which was a sign that America could be reasonable about Asian ambitions. That is why the negotiations continued in good faith for so long, and collapsed only when the American position on China became rocklike and all compromise was rejected.

CHAPTER ONE

Preparing for War

In the spring of 1941 a British observer noted with great interest President Franklin D. Roosevelt's acuity in following the shifts in the trend of American public opinion.

"I have been so struck by the way you have led public opinion by allowing it to get ahead of you," he wrote.

That observation was not quite correct. One of President Roosevelt's strongest qualities was his ability to read the American mind through study of public opinion polls and the words of national leaders. But Roosevelt was not actually behind the public; he was out in front, shaping American attitudes in speeches and with actions. What he did not do was take precipitate action without previous planning and full explanation of his reasoning to the public.

He knew that the majority of people in the United States were opposed to American entry into the European war. The feeling that America had been used by the British in the First World War remained. But by 1940 the horrors visited on Europe by Hitler were beginning to be known, and it was becoming apparent that this war was unlike that of 1914–18. The plucky belligerence of the British was becoming appreciated, and their difficulties created more sympathy in America than had existed for a long time.

As far as Japan was concerned, the Chinese colonies in America did all they could to drum up support for China. Japanese army arrogance in such places as Shanghai did even more, and by 1940 Japan was perceived almost everywhere in America as the coming enemy.

As to defenses, in 1939 Puerto Rico was made a separate department of the military, but Alaska remained under the

9

Ninth Corps area. (The corps areas moved from east to west on the American continent.) General John L. DeWitt was the commander of the Ninth Corps and also of the Fourth Army. There was no unity of command between army and navy—that would have to wait for the Pearl Harbor disaster when, although Washington threw Admiral Husband E. Kimmel and General Walter Short to the wolves, the high commands of army and navy began to realize that if Hawaii had been organized under one command, the disaster might never have taken place.

In the spring of 1941, for defense purposes the continental United States was organized into four areas, of which the West Coast was one, called the Western Defense Command. Alaska was included in this command, and so was the Aleutian Island chain as part of Alaska.

For many years the American presence in Asia had been developed by the American navy. The Great White Fleet that had sailed across the Pacific to Japan in the administration of President Theodore Roosevelt was followed by many other such visits. Each year the Asiatic Fleet paid courtesy visits to Japan, Singapore, Haiphong, Hong Kong, Batavia, and other Far Eastern ports. Every spring the U.S. Fleet (which would be split into Atlantic and Pacific Fleets) staged a Fleet Problem, usually in the Eastern Pacific. The navy was very careful, particularly in the middle and later 1930s, not to cross the International Date Line in these maneuvers, lest Japan be aroused. In 1932 the maneuvers were held in the Eastern Pacific; in 1933 between Hawaii and California; in 1934 on the two sides of the Panama Canal; in 1935 in a triangle between Puget Sound in Washington, the Aleutians, and Hawaii; in 1936 in the Pacific near the Panama Canal; and in 1937 and 1938 in the Hawaii area. The maneuvers were moved to the Caribbean in 1939, but in 1940 they were again returned to the Pacific between Hawaii and the Alaskan frontier. It was remarkable that the American navy would never bring the maneuvers west, which it had a perfect right to do, with bases at Wake Island, Guam, the Western Aleutians, and the Philippines in the Western Pacific, and Midway not far from the International Date-Line on the east. It was a considered policy:

don't arouse Japan. Every year some American naval vessels paid courtesy calls at Yokohama or Nagasaki. The navy sent American naval officers to study the Japanese language in Japan, and the Japanese sent naval officers to study in America. Admiral Isoroku Yamamoto had a stint at Harvard University, and so did many other Japanese. Those Japanese who came to America were generally well-liked and always well-behaved.

But the Americans who studied language in Japan were too few. Only 36 Japanese language officers were generated in 20 years of the program. Only in 1941 when life became very tenuous in the Pacific did the navy devote proper attention to the Japanese language program. Then it opened a Japanese language school that began to train hundreds of men and women in this difficult language.

The shadows of World War I hung over the navy for a long time. The attempt to limit naval armament in 1922 was continued until 1936 when the Japanese let the last treaty expire and began a serious shipbuilding program. In the first years of the 1920s the United States was scrapping ships. Only in 1933, when Franklin D. Roosevelt became President, did the navy begin a building program to modernize the navy. His interest in the navy went back to the First World War, when he was Assistant Secretary of the Navy. He continued that interest, and in 1934 Congress provided for the replacement of obsolete naval vessels by new construction, but the American navy was under strength, and the ships operated with about 80 percent of their expected complement.

The naval arms race really began in earnest in 1936 when the Japanese took the wraps off. The Germans did, too, but Germany, even with its latest big battleships, cruisers, and pocket battleships, did not pretend to be a major naval power. Japan did, and intended that its fleet should dominate the Pacific. In 1938 the Americans and British responded by agreeing to raise the size of battleships from 35,000 tons to 45,000 tons, but the Japanese were way ahead of them. They had already laid down hulls for three 63,700-ton vessels, two of which became the battleships *Yamato* and *Musashi*, and the third, the carrier *Shinano*. In fact, the treaty strength stipulated in 1920 was not achieved by the United States Navy until 1943.

But the most inadequate part of the naval program between the wars related to the naval bases. Only in 1938 did this become a serious matter for concern. That year Congress directed the navy to appoint a board of officers to study the problem. The Hepburn Board then brought in its recommendations in 1939, providing for improvement of the defenses of Alaska and the Aleutians and also of the naval air facilities at Ford Island in Pearl Harbor and Kaneohe on the north shore of Oahu. Midway and Wake islands had been long neglected. In 1939 the Hepburn report advocated their buildup as air bases and submarine bases. Guam, which had begun as a naval coaling station, was not much better in 1938. The Hepburn Board suggested the buildup of Guam to the point where its garrison could hold out against attack until help could arrive from the American mainland.

This was never done, the failure representing a difference of opinion within the navy as to defense capabilities and methods in case of a Pacific war. For a number of years, army and navy planners had agreed on one matter: the western Pacific was indefensible against a sustained Japanese attack unless the United States was willing to rush major support to the area. In that case, a built-up Guam could be defended, and in the Philippines, the Manila Bay region could be held until assistance arrived. The officers who shared this view believed that a strong air and submarine base at Guam would do much to counter the use the Japanese were expected to make of the Bonin, Mariana, Caroline, and Marshall islands. To these officers Guam was a first line of defense, which could be reinforced by units coming from Wake Island and Midway. The Hepburn Board dusted off some previous studies, made by the navy before the Washington Naval Treaty of 1922 forbade such development. But many in the navy had lived with the treaty limitations for so long that they had become sort of second nature. And when the Hepburn Board noted in 1939 that "Guam is adapted naturally to development as a major advanced fleet base," the navy was not ready for that sort of thinking. Ultimately Congress accepted the Hepburn

Board recommendations regarding Alaska, Oahu, Midway, and Wake, but not Guam. Since nothing was done about Guam, the buildup of Wake was less effective, and the state of mind within the navy about Wake tended to be negative except for some far-seeing officers. As for Guam, the fortification did not pass because many in Congress were afraid that to do anything at all would be to provoke Japan. So the United States was in the odd position of failing to protect its own possessions to appease Japan. As U.S. naval historian Samuel Eliot Morison put it, if the Hepburn Board recommendations about Guam had been followed and a major base established there, the whole pattern of the Pacific war might have been altered.

CHAPTER TWO

Defense of Hawaii

At the time of the Japanese attack in December 1941 America's two major outposts were Hawaii and the Panama Canal Zone. The army had the primary responsibility for the protection of both. Army officials were so proud of their defenses of Hawaii in 1941 that they called Oahu island "the greatest fortress in the world."

The army defense of Hawaii began just after the United States annexed the Hawaiian Islands in the summer of 1898. After the Russo-Japanese war, friction between the Japanese and the Americans began, triggered by the successful effort of President Theodore Roosevelt, who negotiated the Treaty of Portsmouth that ended the war, to deprive Japan of a large cash payment in reparations. The Japanese military had nearly bankrupted the Japanese government with this war and was counting on the money to finance military expansion. Instead the military was severely curtailed by the Japanese government, a fact for which the army in particular did not forgive the United States. The development of the ill-feeling caused each nation to begin to look on the other as its primary opponent in the Pacific although there was actually no conflict of interests.

This growing distrust caused the American army and navy to agree to make Oahu a fortress, and a major naval base, which the army would protect. The army increased its Hawaii garrison and in 1913 established the Hawaiian Department as an independent command under the War Department. After World War I, about 11 percent of the American army was stationed on Oahu. Formidable defenses were built on the south shore of the island to protect

Pearl Harbor and Honolulu, including air defenses that were developed to the state of the art. The army mission in Hawaii was defined in 1920 as the defense of Pearl Harbor against invasion by enemy expeditionary forces and an enemy fleet and damage from naval or aerial bombardment or by enemy sympathizers. The last item was an indication of the military feeling against the Japanese who had come to Hawaii to work in the sugar fields and remained to become the most significant part of the population. Whenever the army thought about the Japanese living in Hawaii or the Philippines, they thought about sabotage. The only logical reason for this was the tendency of the Japanese to clannishness and the imperfect understanding by the original Japanese settlers of American ways and language. They tended to read Japanese newspapers, listen to Japanese radio, and pay particular attention to sports and other events in Japan. Their children, however, the American Nisei (second generation), embraced their new homeland with open arms and wanted nothing more than to integrate into American society, a process encouraged officially in the schools but denied in the society of the islands.

The army mission in Hawaii was particularly single-minded until 1941. Until then the army did virtually nothing to build up defenses of the other Hawaiian islands. Only in February 1941 did General George C. Marshall broaden the army responsibility. By that time the navy was using other Hawaiian islands, such as Kahoolawe as a target range and Maui as a sometime base. But both army and navy high commands were certain that there would never be an attack on Hawaii as long as the Pacific Fleet was based there.

Sabotage continued to be the War Department's primary worry about Hawaii. By 1941 the largest single group of people in the islands were people of Japanese ancestry, 37 percent of the total population of 423,000. On Kauai and Hawaii island the Japanese outnumbered the Caucasians by three to one. On Oahu the two races were roughly evenly split. In the islands by that time more than three-quarters of the Japanese were American citizens, but they were still deeply distrusted by the military. The feeling was so strong that the authorities planned immediately to institute martial law on the outbreak of any hostilities.

The army headquarters in Hawaii was at Fort Shafter in Honolulu but the main body of troops was stationed at Schofield Barracks on the plateau between the two mountain ranges. The principal force was the Hawaii Division, which went back to 1921. If there was to be an invasion of Oahu, the military said, it would almost certainly come along the northwest coast. So their plans were based on that assumption. Such invasion would be resisted by the army and the army air force, whose two principal bases were Hickam Field, adjoining Pearl Harbor, and Wheeler Field on the plateau next to Schofield Barracks. Hickam was the bomber base; Wheeler was the fighter base.

When war came to Europe in 1939, the army commander in Hawaii, Major General Charles D. Herron, expressed total confidence in the army's ability to defend Oahu against all comers. The encircling reefs, the mountainous coast, the heavy fortifications of the south shore, and the presence of the division seemed guarantee enough. His only concern was air attacks from the sea by aircraft carrier, but he tended to disregard that threat because the bombers at Hickam Field would attack them before they could ever get near the island.

Because the Washington Naval Treaty of 1921 had forbidden the development of new bases to the west of Hawaii in the Pacific, the military concentrated on building up the Oahu base. The navy by 1938 had spent $75 million on this project, and the army had spent about twice as much to build protection.

The navy and the army had different concepts of the manner in which a war with Japan might develop. The navy planned the launching of an offensive from Hawaii through the Central Pacific. The army believed this to be unrealistic and instead wanted to concentrate on defense of Hawaii and the Panama Canal Zone. After much discussion the Orange Plan for war against Japan was revised in 1938 in an uneasy compromise between these two positions.

In 1935 the army placed Oahu at the top of its priority list and increased the garrison from 14,000 to 21,000 men. That year Major General Hugh A. Drum, who was then commander in Hawaii, had recommended that all the Hawaiian Islands should be defended. He asked for 26 of the new B-17 Flying Fortresses then being developed and proposed the building of bases for them on Hawaii Island and Kauai. He also wanted troops to be stationed on the outer islands. These proposals were rejected by the War Department.

After a long maritime strike in 1936 and 1937 General Drum renewed his request on the basis of safety for Oahu. That island produced only 15 percent of its food, but if communications were maintained with the other islands, on an emergency basis at least, adequate food could be assured.

Again the War Department rejected General Drum's request. The army planned for a wartime garrison of 100,000 men in Hawaii, but they would all remain on Oahu. It was the navy's job to protect the outlying islands. The army's job was to protect fortress Oahu.

Late in 1937 Colonel Edward M. Markham conducted a new survey of Hawaiian defenses at the request of President Roosevelt. He agreed with General Drum that the Pearl Harbor base needed to be made as impregnable as possible. But he saw new difficulties because of the enormous development in air power in the past few years. He was concerned lest an enemy seize Hawaii and make it a base for assault on the continental United States and the Panama Canal. He pointed out that the Japanese had eight carriers either in operation or under construction. How easy it would be for them to approach Oahu from the northeast, move into the island above the Koolawe mountains which were usually covered with clouds, and swoop down on Pearl Harbor. Since local ground defenses and air defenses would thus be without warning (this was before radar), he assumed that the army would increase the air forces of the island to provide for enough bombers to make constant air searches out 600 or 700 miles to prevent surprise attack.

And Colonel Markham made a remarkable prediction:

> War with Japan will be precipitated without notice. One of the most obvious and vital lessons of history is that Japan will pick its own time for conflict. The very

form of its government lends itself to such action in that its military and naval forces can, under the pretext of emergency, initiate and prosecute military and naval operations actions independently of civil control. If and when hostilities develop between Japan and the United States, there can be little doubt that the Hawaiian Islands will be the initial scene of action, and that Japan will apply its available manpower and resources in powerful and determined attacks against these islands.

But the powers that be were not listening. By 1938 the War Department and the Roosevelt administration were focusing their attention on Europe, where Hitler held center stage. The thinking in Washington was that Oahu already had plenty of strong defenses and that concentration must now be made on the Atlantic and Latin America.

In 1939 the War Department heeded Markham's warning enough to recommend increase of the air force planes in Hawaii to 250, with 124 of them to be bombers. (Colonel Markham had recommended at least 350 planes to face an attack expected by about 375 Japanese planes.) The U. S. Army Air Force seemed to recognize the need to have search forces moving out as much as 1,000 miles and to launch air strikes against possible attackers at 600 or 700 miles from the islands.

But later that year the war plans division came up with some new ideas. First, they did not expect the Japanese to attack with more than two carriers. Second, they decided that long-range reconnaissance was a navy mission, not an army mission. On this basis the army reconsidered and allocated not quite 200 planes to Hawaii, only 68 of them bombers. The bombers were to be used for reconnaissance only if the navy was absent or asked for help.

These two attitudes remained a basis for army thinking through 1941.

What the Hawaiian command had at the beginning of 1941 was a mixed collection of 115 combat planes, all of them obsolete. By December 7, they had 12 B-17 bombers, but only six of them were operational.

When the European war began, the United States Fleet

was based on the West Coast at San Diego, with the advance base then being Pearl Harbor. But after the maneuvers of April 1940 Admiral James O. Richardson was ordered to stay at Pearl Harbor as a deterrent to the Japanese. After the fall of France, the naval command in Washington considered the transfer of the U. S. Fleet to the Atlantic. General Marshall objected, and on June 17, 1940, he alerted the Hawaii Department and the Panama Canal Zone Department of the army to the danger of raids from Japan. He feared a raid on Hawaii only if the fleet had departed.

General Herron reacted immediately to the alert. He ordered 24-hour staffing of all observation posts and issued live ammunition to the antiaircraft gun crews with instructions to fire first and ask later about unidentified aircraft. Aircraft at Hickam and Wheeler fields were dispersed and the army took over the inshore air patrol. Admiral Richardson then began some long-range patrols. These lasted for several months, but toward the end of 1940 a more relaxed atmosphere returned. When President Roosevelt decided in July to keep the fleet in Hawaii, General Marshall's worries had really ended.

At this time the United States was moving from neutrality to "nonbelligerency" in the Atlantic. It was important that nothing untoward happen in the Pacific, but at the same time President Roosevelt felt the need to warn the Japanese of serious American concern over the Rome-Berlin-Tokyo axis that had just come into being. He wanted to send a National Guard regiment to reinforce Hawaii, but the army persuaded him that this would be wasteful and confusing. Instead, he ordered sent a regiment of antiaircraft artillery, the first National Guard unit to leave the continental United States for duty in World War II.

But no one in the army seemed to notice that at the end of 1940 Admiral Richardson discontinued his long-range air patrols from Hawaii.

In January 1941 Admiral Richardson suggested that the danger to Hawaii would come from a surprise attack against the American fleet at Pearl Harbor, and he suggested that the army should improve its air raid warning network and increase its fighter plane contingent and its antiaircraft artillery. At about that time President Roosevelt suggested that Japan even then could be planning an attack on Pearl Harbor. The Army war plans division then suggested that Hawaii be put on a war basis and be reinforced with B-17s. General Marshall arranged for the dispatch of 81 fighter planes to Oahu.

In February 1941 the army and navy commands in Hawaii changed. Admiral Husband E. Kimmel became commander of the Pacific Fleet and Lieutenant General Walter C. Short became commander of the Army Hawaiian Department.

By April 1941 the fears about Japanese action were submerged in Washington to greater concerns about the situation of Britain and the war in Europe. General Marshall expressed himself as quite satisfied with the state of Hawaii defenses. The army had 55 more P-40s, and 35 more B-17s were supposed to be sent to Oahu. General Marshall told Secretary of War Stimson that he thought Hawaii was impregnable: "With our heavy bombers and our fine pursuit planes, the land force could put up such a defense that the Japs wouldn't dare attack Hawaii, particularly such a long distance from home."

The real danger, said General Marshall at that time, was from sabotage, and the government should set up a military government of Hawaii before undertaking any involvement in the Far East.

As for the possibility of Japanese attack, it would have to be a carrier attack.

"Carrier raids by the Japanese involve jeopardizing naval units that will not be lightly undertaken. To meet these raids our bombardment (planes) protected by pursuit aviation, the latter operating from advanced fields on the islands of Kauai and Hawaii, can cover a radius from Oahu of approximately 400 miles." This opinion was then generally shared. So the attitude of Washington to Hawaii defense was more confidence than ever.

In the spring of 1941 the army and navy in Hawaii agreed that the responsibility for long-range reconnaissance rested with the navy, but army and navy continued to operate separately.

Instead of the 35 B-17s that had been promised, in May

1941, Hawaii got only 21 altogether. General Marshall with-held the others because of the critical outlook in the European war.

The euphoria continued. The commander of the Hawaiian air force said confidently that one 35-plane group of B-17s would be enough to finish off six enemy carriers. What he wanted was bombers for reconnaissance, and he wanted 180 heavy bombers. His request was warmly endorsed by General Short, but all that Hawaii could get was a promise of perhaps 250 heavy army bombers by the middle of 1942.

What was really lacking in Hawaii was an air raid early warning system. Radar was very much in the development stage in the United States, and the army on Oahu was operating only five mobile sets. A sixth, located at Opana on the northern tip of the island, was put in action in November 1941. Three bigger fixed sets arrived in November, but the mountaintop sites were not prepared to receive them. The mobile sets had a range of 75 to 125 miles. In an exercise in November the radars picked up an "enemy" force 80 miles out, and the American fighters intercepted them 30 miles from Oahu. But the radar sets were operated only about four hours a day, and that for training only.

As for antiaircraft defenses, the army had 60 mobile and 26 fixed three-inch guns, 109 antiaircraft machine guns, and twenty 37-mm guns. But the ammunition for the 37-mm guns did not arrive until December 5, 1941, and most of the other ammunition was in the ordnance depot. The army would need several hours of warning to get the guns supplied with ammunition. Also, because of the ammunition shortage, virtually no training was conducted with live ammunition.

General Short had seen the need for dispersal of aircraft on the army fields and had begun to build bunkers, but on November 27, 1941, the army declared that planes should be bunched up and guarded against sabotage, so the bunkers were never put in use.

General Short decided to garrison the outer islands, largely as a measure against sabotage on the airfields that were used by the fighter planes. So battalions of troops were sent to Hawaii and Kauai, and smaller units went to Maui and Molokai. In the year before the Pearl Harbor attack the garrison was increased to 43,000 troops and the army seemed to believe that that was quite enough and that all the defenses of Hawaii were totally secure.

In the first half of 1941 American attention was focused on the Atlantic, where the United States Navy was becoming ever more involved in the war against the U-boats. But in July 1941 Washington learned that the Japanese were planning further military adventures. Through breach of the Japanese codes the navy learned that Japan had decided to strike south to secure the natural resources it needed.

The American reaction was twofold. First, Washington applied the most stringent economic sanctions against Japan, in the hope of forcing the Japanese to a different course. The result was precisely the opposite; American cutoff of oil and other materials simply convinced the Japanese that the only way to secure the resources they needed was to capture them. So unless the United States changed its policy, war had become inevitable.

The second Washington move, by the army, was to decide to defend the Philippines, and therefore to strengthen its defenses. The decision was made to send large numbers of B-17 bombers to the Philippines. Also, the United States would need to strengthen the Midway and Wake Island bases that formed the route to Manila. The plans and preparations could not come to fruition before 1942, but the army did not expect the Japanese to strike before that time. The concept that the Japanese might try a carrier raid on Oahu as outlined by Colonel Markham was completely dismissed. Army and navy leaders had both convinced themselves that an attack on Oahu was so improbable as to be ridiculous. What worried both army and navy now was the possibility of sabotage by the Japanese in the Hawaiian islands. As General Marshall put it: "I fully anticipated a terrific effort to cripple everything out there by sabotage."

Twice in July the army sent warnings to Hawaii commander General Short. He responded by putting the army forces on full alert and staging war games. He put army guards on a 24-hour basis at military and public utility installations, on highway bridges, and along the Honolulu waterfront. In the fall the army and the navy parted company in their assessments of the dangers. The navy issued its first warning to fleet commanders that the Japanese might soon initiate military action. The army did not believe it, and so sent messages to General Short and General Douglas MacArthur, commander of American forces in the Philippines, that while tension was high between the two countries, there did not seem to be any abrupt change in foreign policy in the offing. In Hawaii the vital installations continued to be under 24-hour-a-day guard. As of November 21, 1941, President Roosevelt was still not sure that the Japanese were not bluffing. The military opinion in Washington was that the Japanese were too weak and too greatly extended in China and Manchuria to launch any new military enterprises.

No further information was forthcoming from the army in Washington until November 27. In fact, on that day Admiral Kimmel; Admiral Claude Bloch, the commander of the Fourteenth Naval District; and General Short spent three hours discussing a Washington proposal that they reinforce Midway and Wake islands by sending 50 of their most modern fighter planes. They also discussed bombs and bombers. General Short said the army could not spare any 500-pound bombs for Midway or Wake. Hawaii had only six B-17s in commission. In the course of the discussion Admiral Kimmel turned to his war plans officer, Captain Charles H. McMorris, and asked him what were the chances of a Japanese surprise attack on Hawaii.

"None," said Captain McMorris.

Then came a "war warning" from Washington. In the warning given by General Marshall to the Philippines, General MacArthur was instructed "to undertake reconnaissance and such other measures as you may deem necessary but those measures should be carried out so as not, repeat not to alarm the civil population or to disclose intent."

Washington's warning to Hawaii to General Short simply told him to guard against sabotage. The next day he issued Alert No. 1, which assumed sabotage and unrest but no external threat.

On November 29 the War Department announced that it

intended to defend Christmas and Canton islands, which was a departure from previous army feelings about the Western Pacific. All this while B-17s from the mainland were coming through Hawaii, where they were made combat-ready and armed and sent on to the Philippines.

By that time the Honolulu press was reporting the impending rupture of relations and Japanese warlike moves. At this time the Japanese force that would strike Hawaii was in Tanken Bay in the Kuriles, prepared to move across the Pacific.

The general public seemed to be ahead of "informed opinion" about what the future held. The lead editorial in the *Honolulu Advertiser* on December 3 said, "Unless there is an immediate and complete reversal of Tokyo policy, the die is cast. Japan and America will travel down the road to war."

But in Washington army military intelligence announced that for the next four months at least the only power capable of launching large-scale offensives was Germany.

In Hawaii it was business as usual. More than 24,000 people turned out on the afternoon of Saturday, December 6, to watch the University of Hawaii football team beat Willamette University, 20 to 6. There was no attempt to integrate army and navy defenses, although a plan had been set up to do so in time of emergency. The navy had 50 patrol bombers in service but did not increase its long-range patrols. The planes that were supposed to come to Hawaii for that purpose would not arrive for another year.

Then came the Japanese attack on Pearl Harbor. After the attack the army placed a new priority on air power for Hawaii. As soon as Admiral William F. Halsey arrived at Pearl Harbor with the carrier *Enterprise,* he moved to go out and find the Japanese, but nobody knew where they were and he searched south rather than north, while the Japanese fleet steamed swiftly northwest on the route home.

Then army and navy finally could agree on joint operations for long-range search, and searches began out 700 miles in all directions. The whole question of air search came under review. The navy transferred three squadrons of patrol planes from the Atlantic, and the army employed its bombers for search.

General Marshall ordered the army air forces to build up the bomber strength to a full group of heavy bombers and two groups of fighter planes. The bombers were easy to come by because the attack on the Philippines had stopped the flow of B-17s there. By December 21 the bomber group of 43 planes was established on Oahu.

The navy response to the Pearl Harbor attack was the transfer of three battleships from the Atlantic Fleet to the Pacific. On December 9 the army plan to reinforce the Philippines was discarded. The convoy bound for Manila was called back to Honolulu by presidential order and diverted to Australia. The whole perimeter defense program was in flux.

In Hawaii a few hours after the attack took place, the army began to impose tight controls on public and private life. A first step was to find all the still and motion pictures made of the attack, except those taken by the navy, and confiscate them. Before noon army intelligence had imposed tight censorship on Hawaii to prevent any unauthorized transmission of information about the attack or about Oahu's defenses.

Hawaii Governor Joseph B. Poindexter went on the air to calm the public and announce that he was putting Hawaii's emergency act (M-Day Act) into effect. He was cut off the air by the army, on the excuse that a Japanese task force was using radio beams to navigate their ships.

The real reason was that the army intended to put military law into effect. The M-Day Act had been an attempt by the Hawaiian legislature in October 1941 to avoid military rule. General Short would not accept it. He was still talking about sabotage although there was no sabotage. The general called on Governor Poindexter and told him he was going to institute military law. The governor called President Roosevelt to forestall the measure, but Roosevelt approved the invocation of military law, so Hawaii became an occupied territory. That day under duress the governor signed the papers giving the general control of Hawaii, suspending the writ of habeas corpus, and giving the general full judicial as well as executive power. So Hawaiians lost their American civil rights at 3:45 on the afternoon of December 7, 1941.

That morning General Short had ordered the evacuation from military installations of all dependents. The intelligence staff began to round up "suspicious" characters, and by December 10 had arrested 482 Japanese, Germans, and Italians, about 10 percent of them American citizens.

Under military law the army ordered a complete blackout and curfew every night from 6 P.M. Private cars were barred from the highways. All bars were closed. The sale of liquor was forbidden. Civil courts were suspended and military courts substituted. All schools were closed. All food sales were suspended pending an inventory of stock. Gasoline was rationed.

In the beginning the Hawaiian public accepted these restrictions as necessary, but as time went on and there was no sabotage and no unrest, the haste of the army became apparent, and the public began to complain, to no avail. Martial law remained until after the battle of Midway in June 1942, and the army continued to worry about sabotage and espionage that never happened. The people of Hawaii did not regain their full civil rights until the last of October 1944, when the war in Europe was virtually won and the war in the Pacific was going into its final stages.

In the first few days after the Pearl Harbor raid the army wanted to initiate a mass evacuation of the Japanese from Hawaii. That would have been quite an undertaking, reminiscent of the mass deportations of the Stalin purges or of the Nazi pattern of behavior. Fortunately wiser heads prevailed, and since there was no disturbance by the Japanese citizens of Hawaii, there was no excuse for this racist behavior.

The food stock inventory showed that Hawaii had a 37-day supply of food on hand. Congress appropriated $35 million to finance shipments of food on an emergency basis, and as soon as the submarine scare vanished on the West Coast several months later, the food chain became more or less normal. The Japanese, after sinking a few ships in the first days after the Pearl Harbor attack and sending submarines to scout the Aleutians and the West Coast of the

United States never began warfare against American commerce, although this could have been one of their most effective ways of hurting the American defenses.

The American government claimed proudly that never during the war had it invoked military censorship, but this was not true in Hawaii. Tight military censorship of mail was begun, along with censorship of newspapers and radio station broadcasts. Within three days foreign language newspapers were closed down, as well as labor and Communist newspapers. Ultimately the army gave up this control but throughout the war continued a tight rein on the information processes.

Hardly had the Japanese planes disappeared over the horizon than the army began an enormous building program to repair the air installations and build anew. In a few weeks 20,000 civilian workers were employed on army projects in Oahu.

The big change in the defense pattern of Hawaii came on December 17, when Admiral Kimmel and General Short were relieved of command. At that time the command of all defense activities was put in the hands of the commander in chief of the Pacific Fleet, Admiral Chester W. Nimitz, who would take over as soon as he could get there.

CHAPTER THREE

The Western Perimeter

At the time of the Pearl Harbor attack the Japanese had sent 25 submarines to Hawaii to collect intelligence, launch five midget submarines toward the harbor, and lurk outside to sink any men-of-war that came out.

After the attack some of the submarines went to the West Coast, but nine of them remained in Hawaiian waters. One of their tasks was to try to discover precisely what damage had been done by the attacking force. The reports of the pilots were fragmentary and often contradictory. So early on the morning of December 18 the submarine *I-7* launched a reconnaissance plane that flew over Pearl Harbor and reported back to Tokyo. The next day Imperial General Headquarters announced that eight battleships, four cruisers, and two destroyers had been sunk or heavily damaged. Damage had also been done to four other cruisers and other vessels. They had to guess at the destruction to aircraft and they guessed high: 450 aircraft destroyed on the ground and 14 in the air. That figure was about twice the total number of planes in Hawaii at the time of the attack.

The Japanese plane was not seen, nor was one that flew over Pearl Harbor on the night of January 6, 1942.

One reason that the army and navy were apprehensive about another raid or an invasion attempt was the continued presence of these submarines. One of the submarines moved to Kahului on Maui and on the night of December 15 fired 10 shells from its deck gun into the harbor. Three shells hit a pineapple cannery. On the night of December 30 submarines also shelled Hilo on the island of Hawaii, Nawiliwili on Kauai, and Kahului again. So for several weeks Hawaiians waited for the other shoe to drop, but that was the end of the attacks in the islands. From that point on the submarines that came to American waters cruised off the coast of the mainland and the Aleutians.

The Japanese then proceeded to try to wipe out the American presence in the Western Pacific. At dawn on December 8 Japanese dive bombers and fighters from the carrier *Ryujo* began the assault on the Philippines with an attack on the seaplane tender *William B. Preston* in Davao Gulf. Two of the *Preston*'s planes were destroyed at their moorings. From Taiwan airfields Japanese army bombers attacked Baguio in northern Luzon and Tugugarao airfield. A huge fleet of nearly 200 navy bombers and fighters from Taiwan also attacked Nichols and Clark fields and destroyed about half the American air force planes there. As in Hawaii the American aircraft were lined up neatly on the aprons and heavily guarded, for the great concern was sabotage.

On December 8 the Japanese also landed an assault force on Batan Island in Bashi Channel, as the first step in their amphibious assault on Luzon. They thought they might need to build airfields there to support the landings a little later. But as it turned out the attacks on the Clark Field complex had so mangled the American air force that these fields were not necessary and two days later the Japanese landed and seized Camiguin Island, where they established a seaplane base. That day the Japanese air forces attacked Cavite naval base in Manila and landed troops at Aparri on the north coast of Luzon and took over the airstrip there for support of their ground forces. Soon Japanese army units were landing at several points in the Philippines, and on December 21 landed a major amphibious force at Lingayen Gulf. Altogether they made nine amphibious landings in the Philippines. The drive for Manila was then on. By Christmas the Japanese were fast approaching, and on December 27 General MacArthur declared Manila to be an open city and began his retreat into the Bataan Peninsula, where he intended to fight until help could come from the United States.

The Japanese also cast their eyes on the other American bases in the Pacific. First was Guam, that island in the Marianas group that the navy had wanted to fortify, but did not because of congressional concern over irritating the Japanese. In the fall of 1941 Guam was totally defenseless. Realizing this, Captain G. J. McMillin, the governor of the island, evacuated all the women and children from Guam in mid-October. On December 8, then, the island garrison consisted of 30 naval officers, six warrant officers, five navy nurses, 230 enlisted men, seven marine officers, one warrant officer, 145 marines, and 246 members of the Chamorro Insular Force. The largest weapon on the island was a .30-caliber machine gun. The island's naval defenses consisted of three small patrol boats and one old tanker. What could have been a highly fortified base to hold out in the middle of the Marianas islands was then ripe for capture.

Japanese planes from Saipan began bombing the marine headquarters on Guam on the morning of December 8. They also sank the patrol boat *Penguin*. For two days the Japanese bombed and strafed the island. On the night of December 8 a dugout canoe landed with a party of Chamorros from Saipan who were sent ahead by the Japanese to be interpreters for the invasion force. They were arrested. They informed the Americans that the Japanese would land the next morning on the beach east of Agana. The marines thought it was a ruse, but the place turned out to be correct although the landings were not made until the following day, December 10. Five thousand Japanese landed that day. The fighting force came ashore on the beach at Agana. They marched on the plaza, where the Insular Force and some American marines and navy sailors put up strong resistance and drove the Japanese back to the beach. The Americans lost 17 men but the Japanese lost many more. But the governor, hearing of the other landings in force, realized that there was no point in sacrificing more lives and so decided to surrender. The Japanese came to Government House, where the governor negotiated a promise that the Chamorros' civil rights would be respected and the military personnel would be treated as prisoners of war. He signed the surrender document, and the Stars and Stripes was lowered and the Rising Sun flag was run up the pole. A handful of navy sailors escaped to the hills where they were hidden and protected by the Chamorros until the return of the Americans in the summer of 1944.

What a different story it might have been at Wake, the atoll that historian Samuel Eliot Morison called "the ideal fixed aircraft carrier."

Wake is located 1,000 miles from Midway and 1,300 miles from Guam. The navy wanted to fortify Guam to complete the string of bases that could threaten the Japanese in their Marshall Islands mandate. Guam is only 620 miles from Kwajalein Atoll. With Guam, Wake, and Midway in American hands, the Japanese could be hamstrung in the Central Pacific. Now Guam was gone, but after the Pearl Harbor attack Wake remained American.

For several years Wake had been the site of a Pan American Airways base for its China Clipper service to the Orient. When Congress had declined to strengthen Guam in 1939 some officers tended to write Wake off also as indefensible without Guam, but others disagreed. The Hepburn Board had recommended that the navy fortify Wake, as well as Midway, as air and submarine bases. In 1940 Congress accepted that idea and voted the appropriation. In 1941 the airfield was built on Wake Island.

Lest there be any doubts in Washington about Wake, Admiral Kimmel, the commander in chief of the Pacific Fleet, in the spring of 1941 urged that strong defensive measures be taken at Wake. If it fell into the hands of the Japanese, he warned, it would be a serious obstacle to operations of the American navy in the Central Pacific.

"To deny Wake to the enemy, without occupying it ourselves," the admiral said, "would be difficult. To recapture it, if the Japanese should seize it in the early period of hostilities, would require operations of some magnitude."

The admiral predicted that one of the initial Japanese operations would be directed against Wake, and that it would be carried out by the Japanese Fourth Fleet's amphibious group. If Wake were fortified and defended, then it might be possible to draw the Japanese navy out to fight there.

The Japanese had been watching Wake for some time, and planes from the Marshall Island bases checked on what was happening there. They proposed to capture Wake as well as Guam and then move on to Midway. After that, perhaps Hawaii. Certainly the Aleutians. For the Wake operation, Admiral Kimmel was exactly right: the Japanese had selected the Fourth Fleet at Truk to do the job. As the Japanese ships steamed for Pearl Harbor, Vice Admiral Inouye was standing by at Truk waiting for X-Day to dispatch the fleet amphibious command.

Earlier in the year, the navy had agreed with Admiral Kimmel's assessment of the need to fortify and defend Wake, and that summer of 1941 a detachment of the Marine First Defense Battalion was sent to Wake.

The Marine Defense Battalions had recently been developed for the specific purpose of defending atolls. Its armament consisted of half a dozen five-inch guns, a dozen three-inch antiaircraft guns, a machine gun group with forty-eight .50-caliber machine guns and forty .30-caliber machine guns, and a thousand officers and men.

By November Major James P. Devereux had arrived with more men but it was still not a complete battalion. Late in November 1941 a naval party also went to Wake to set up the air station for the PBY flying boat base that would be installed there. Marine Fighter Squadron VMF-211 was also stationed at Wake with a dozen Grumman Wildcat fighters. By December 8, 1941, there were on Wake 27 marine corps officers and 422 enlisted men, about 70 navy men, a small army communications unit, and some 1,200 civilians, who were Pan American employees or contractors' workers.

The base was unfinished and had no radar and revetments to protect parked aircraft, but the defense guns were installed, and the marines were there to operate them.

On December 7, which on Wake was the day before the Japanese attack on Pearl Harbor, the China Clipper arrived from the east and at dawn the next morning took off for Guam.

The marines were just finishing breakfast that morning when a message arrived from Pearl Harbor announcing the Japanese air attack. Major Devereux moved into action. The marines grabbed rifles and ammunition and hurried to their duty posts. Aviators warmed up their fighter planes. Civilians started digging foxholes, and the China Clipper turned back from Guam and landed at Wake. The China Clipper pilot, Captain J. H. Hamilton was preparing to fly a patrol out 100 miles around the island to look for the Japanese, and his aircraft was being gassed up. Just then the Japanese bombers arrived, swooping down out of a rain cloud.

The first strike came in at noon. Three V-shaped formations of twin-engined bombers, 12 planes in each V, darted out of the rain clouds, leveled out at 2,000 feet, and made for the airfield. On the field eight F4F Wildcat fighters were being serviced. Four of the planes suffered direct bomb hits and disintegrated. The other four were set afire, and three of them were destroyed but one was salvaged. Twenty-three marine officers and men were killed or mortally wounded. Other Japanese planes in the formation then bombed the Pan American air station, destroying almost all the facilities, including the hotel for Clipper passengers. Ten civilians were killed. The China Clipper, sitting in the lagoon, was strafed but not seriously damaged.

In 10 minutes the air raid was over and the Japanese were heading for home.

That afternoon the China Clipper took off with a full load of civilian passengers and flew for Midway.

Most of the civilians on the island then scattered into the brush and stayed there, but a few volunteers worked all night along with the marines to repair damage done by the bombing.

The next day the Japanese came again. Two of the American fighter planes got into the air and shot down a bomber, and the antiaircraft guns shot down another and damaged several more. But this second bombing attack destroyed the navy radio station and hit the hospital, killing about 60 people, most of them civilians. Major Devereux ordered a new hospital devised in two underground ammunition magazines.

Having a hunch that the next Japanese bombing target would be his five-inch guns of Battery E, Major Devereux then moved the guns from the emplacements to a point 600 yards north.

A flight of 27 bombers came over on December 10. Two Japanese planes were shot down by a marine pilot but the rest concentrated on the empty gun emplacements and on Wilkes Island, where Major Devereux now concluded the Japanese landing force would try to come in. The Japanese blew up a construction dynamite dump; the 125 pounds of dynamite made an impressive explosion, which set off all the ready ammunition in the nearby gun batteries and damaged the guns of Batteries F and L. One marine was killed and another wounded.

That night the Japanese came to Wake. Just after midnight marines on lookout duty reported seeing lights blinking to the south. The moon rose, and then they could see ships approaching Peacock Point. It was the Japanese Fourth Fleet invasion force, commanded by Rear Admiral S. Kajioka, who flew his flag in the light cruiser *Yubari*.

For some reason the Japanese had mixed up all their priorities, perhaps because the capture of Guam had come so easily. For the Guam invasion, against an island that had no weapons, they had used 5,000 troops. For the invasion of Wake they sent only 450 Special Landing Force troops in two transport destroyers, and about three times as many garrison troops, in transports escorted by six destroyers. The light cruisers *Tenryu* and *Tatsuta* comprised the support force.

Two submarines had been hanging about Wake for several days, scouting and reporting.

The Japanese came up steadily and slowly. At about 5 o'clock on the morning of December 11, they swung to port about four miles off Peacock Point, with the *Yubari* in the lead. They began a run along the southern shore of the atoll, moving along Wake Island and next-door Wilkes Island. The three light cruisers opened fire on the shore. They set fire to some oil tanks.

The transports set about getting their troops into the boats and were obviously having difficulty because the sea was very heavy.

Major Devereux cautioned his men not to fire until he ordered. He watched for an hour as the ships moved along. Then at 6:15 the *Yubari* and three destroyers in a column made another turn and came in on a firing run about three miles offshore. Battery A, which was located at Peacock

Point, then opened up its five-inch guns. The shooting was excellent. The guns put at least three shells into the *Yubari* and she turned and went off over the horizon.

Battery L, located at the other end of the atoll, on Wilkes Island, began firing on the destroyers, which were coming up in a column. The five-inch guns hit the *Hyate* with six shells, and she blew up, broke in two, and sank. Battery L fired on the destroyer *Oite* and damaged her, then began shooting at one of the transports. A shell hit the transport. The destroyers began making smoke and both transports got behind the smoke and retired toward the sea. Battery L then shot at a second light cruiser, which was hit and turned away from the island, smoking.

Three of the destroyers had been standing off the island. Now they began a north-south run to fire on Wilkes Island's Battery L and Peale Island's Battery B on Toki Point. The five-inch guns began to fire and the destroyer *Yayoi* was hit. The destroyer threw shells into the island all around the battery and knocked out the fire control communications line. Battery B then shifted fire to another destroyer.

At this time the four remaining American fighters joined the battle, dropping 100-pound fragmentation bombs and strafing. They would make an attack, use up their ammunition, go back to the airfield, land, get more ammunition, and take off again. They damaged the cruisers *Tenryu* and *Tatsuta* and started a fire on a transport. One pilot attacked the destroyer *Kisaragi*. His 100-pound bombs hit the ship's depth charges, but the *Kisaragi*'s antiaircraft guns riddled the plane so that it just made the beach in a crash landing. Another American fighter was starting a run on the *Kisaragi* when her depth charges blew up from the first plane's bombs, and she sank without any survivors.

Admiral Kajioka, having lost two destroyers and suffered damage to several other ships, and seeing the difficulties of getting the men into the boats, decided to retire to Kwajalein, secure reinforcements, and wait for the weather to improve before making another attempt at the invasion.

That morning Major Devereux counted the accomplishments. They had driven off the invasion, sinking two destroyers and killing about 500 Japanese, plus those killed in the other ships. They had lost one man. They had lost two more fighters, but they still had two left, and when the Japanese bombers came over again that day the two fighters shot down two of the 18 Japanese planes. The antiaircraft guns shot down another bomber, and four others limped away smoking.

So Major Devereux and the marines had won the battle of the day and sent the Japanese back where they came from. Now they could relax for a little and wait for the reinforcements from Pearl Harbor that were expected.

Two days after the Pearl Harbor raid, Admiral Kimmel had recalled his letter of the springtime to Washington advocating the defense of Wake Island. He put a plan in motion to defend the island even before the Japanese had made their first attempt at landing.

His objective was not only to save Wake as a vital base on the American perimeter but also to draw out elements of the Japanese fleet and win a victory that would restore American prestige and morale. To relieve Wake he would use all three of the carrier task forces at his disposal: Admiral Halsey's *Enterprise*, Rear Admiral Aubrey W. Fitch's *Saratoga*, and Admiral Wilson Brown's *Lexington*. Thus he would get at the Japanese naval force with American naval force.

The *Lexington* would make a raid on Jaluit atoll in the Marshall Islands. This would keep the Japanese occupied there and also destroy ships and air facilities.

The *Saratoga* would carry out the actual relief of Wake.

The *Enterprise*, which was at sea still looking for the Japanese, would come into Pearl Harbor, refuel, and then go west to Johnston Island to cover Oahu against any surprise and to support Admiral Fitch's main strike with the *Saratoga*.

Although the *Saratoga* task force was newly created it got the task of the relief because it was en route to Pearl Harbor at that moment, carrying Marine Fighter Squadron 222 and all its personnel and equipment, plus 18 Brewster Buffalo fighters.

In addition, the seaplane tender *Tangier* was in Pearl

Harbor, and it was loaded with ammunition and equipment for the marines on Wake Island.

So far the plan seemed workable enough. But then Admiral Kimmel ran into the big difficulty. Who would be in overall command? Admiral Fitch should have been, but he was only a rear admiral, and Brown and Halsey both outranked him. Besides, neither of them would actually be going to Wake. That part and the strike was to be left to Fitch, who was the most experienced of all the navy's carrier admirals, having been an airman since 1930.

Because of the navy seniority system, Kimmel then made a grievous error. He looked around to find a senior officer, and he chose Rear Admiral Frank Jack Fletcher, the commander of Cruiser Division Six. Kimmel put the overall command in the hands of Fletcher, who would go to Wake along with the *Astoria, Minneapolis*, and *San Francisco*. So he was putting what was essentially a carrier operation into the hands of a man who knew virtually nothing about carriers.

It was true that Fletcher had shown outstanding merit in the peacetime navy, but what about his aggressiveness? The wartime navy was quite a different matter, as the Americans would learn soon enough, and men who had excelled in a spit-and-polish peacetime navy did not always have the courage and tenacity to be good fighting men. It took a little dash as well, a little of the Nelson mystique.

Kimmel appointed Fletcher to command the expedition without even finding out how Fletcher felt about the whole enterprise.

What with one problem after another the expedition was delayed. Meanwhile the marines had won the first round at Wake and were now waiting. Admiral Kajioka had gone back to Truk and was assembling a much more powerful force to try once again to assault Wake.

The *Saratoga* came in from the West Coast and fueled. The *Lexington* was supposed to fuel at sea, but the weather was so rough that she could not, and had to come into Pearl Harbor to do the job. Thus, there was more delay.

It was December 14 when the Wake relief force finally

assembled and got moving. Admiral Brown was very nervous about the whole expedition, so just before he sailed Admiral Kimmel gave him permission to change his objective and not bombard Jaluit, or to retire and come home.

On the morning of December 16 three of *Lexington*'s planes reported an enemy carrier about a hundred miles southeast of Pearl Harbor. The scout bombers dropped bombs but they all missed. Admiral Brown sent off an attack of 29 bombers and seven fighters. They found the "carrier," which turned out to be a derelict dynamite barge that had been under tow to Pearl Harbor on December 7 when the Japanese had attacked. The naval tug *Antares* was doing the towing. Coming through the submarine net into Pearl Harbor, the *Antares* had been trailed by a Japanese midget submarine that was then sunk by the destroyer *Ward*. In the confusion the *Antares* had cast off its tow to maneuver, and the barge had drifted out to sea.

On December 17 the *Lexington* group held antiaircraft practice. All their antiaircraft ammunition failed to function. This was unnerving to Admiral Brown.

On December 18 the Pacific Fleet intelligence officer reported that the Japanese had landed perhaps 200 aircraft in the Gilbert Islands. The report was a total exaggeration. The Japanese had actually landed a token force at Tarawa and a small construction group to build a seaplane base at Makin. In order to attack Jaluit, Admiral Brown's ships would have to pass about 100 miles north of Makin. If that were not enough to alarm Admiral Brown, the Pacific Fleet also reported that the commander of the Japanese Sixth Fleet, the submarine command, was at Jaluit. So Admiral Brown had visions of being attacked by 200 airplanes from the Gilberts, and perhaps a half dozen submarines from Jaluit.

Admiral Brown then concluded that he was moving into a Japanese trap.

In the meantime, Admiral Kimmel was relieved as commander in chief of the Pacific Fleet. The word was passed that a new commander would be coming to Pearl Harbor in a few days, but in the interim Vice Admiral W. S. Pye, who was senior officer present at Pearl Harbor, took over command of the fleet.

Admiral Pye knew little about carrier operations, and being thrown into command of the fleet at a time when Admiral Kimmel had just ordered an offensive operation using all three of the fleet's carriers—basically the total striking force—made Admiral Pye feel uncertain.

On December 20 Admiral Brown had just decided that the whole Jaluit operation was too risky and that he would attack Makin instead. Then Brown had new orders from Admiral Pye. The *Lexington* force was to belay the old orders and turn north and support Admiral Fletcher, who was moving in against Wake. This was a sensible decision, which had come from within the Pacific Fleet staff.

Admiral Halsey had entered Pearl Harbor on December 16 and departed again on December 20, and as ordered steamed out 230 miles east of Midway, where he remained for several days, waiting to see if a sea fight developed.

On December 20 the marines at Wake island reported that affairs were progressing very badly there. They had been attacked several times in the past few hours by Japanese bombers. All but two of their fighter planes had been destroyed. They were growing desperate for assistance.

So on December 21 Admiral Fletcher decided that he had to fuel. At 8 P.M. on December 21 the *Saratoga* force was 600 miles from Wake. The next day Fletcher stopped all action and fueled.

The original Japanese invasion force retired to Kwajalein, not to Truk, on December 13 and picked up reinforcements. The two sunk destroyers were replaced. Admiral Kajioka also now had a seaplane tender loaded with more troops, about 2,000 special landing force troops in all, and a minelayer. The cruiser *Yubari* was patched up, and so were the *Tenryu* and *Tatsuta*. In view of what had happened at Wake the last time, Admiral Inouye sent from Truk a strong force, four heavy cruisers and destroyers, which had been used at Guam and were now free. But also from Admiral Nagumo's Pearl Harbor striking force, Admiral Yamamoto detached the carriers *Soryu* and *Hiryu* and the heavy cruisers *Tone* and *Chikuma* to support the Wake Island attack. On December 21 this force launched its first bomber strike on Wake.

Admiral Kajioka left Kwajalein on December 20, expecting to land on Wake before dawn on December 23. At that point Admiral Fletcher's relief force was 600 miles from Wake, and if Admiral Fletcher had steamed ahead he would have been there in plenty of time to be lying in wait for the Japanese. But, instead, he fueled.

So the Japanese were coming.

Nearly every day since the first invasion had been repelled the marines on Wake had been bombed by planes from the Marshalls. For several days the marines had managed to keep two fighters in the air by cannibalizing the remnants of the others.

All the above-ground installations were being destroyed by this constant bombing, which was hard on morale, but morale had a great boost on December 20 when a Catalina flew in with the mail and the news that the Wake Island relief expedition was on its way.

Two hours after the Catalina departed on December 21 the island had the first attack from the carrier planes. The two planes still intact on Wake remained so. One flew off in search of the enemy carriers but did not have enough gas to find them. The other, on the ground, was the object of repeated strafing but was not hit.

On December 22, however, another carrier raid came in. This time the pilots of the marine planes shot down two Zeros, but were themselves shot down in turn. That was the end of the airplanes. The officers and men of VMF-211 then joined the marine ground force as infantrymen.

On the evening of December 22, as Admiral Fletcher was still fueling, the Japanese invasion fleet stood off Wake and made ready to attack the island with a landing the next day. The support force of cruisers and carriers maneuvered about 150 miles from Wake. Here was the opportunity for which Admiral Kimmel had hoped. His three carrier task forces would have been superior in force to the two Japanese carriers, and if it came to a surface battle his cruisers and the Japanese cruisers would have been fairly matched. It was, indeed, the chance for an American victory, if only the carriers had been where they should have been. But Fletcher was fueling.

At 2:30 in the morning of December 23, the Japanese began their assault. Six landing barges, each loaded with 50 men, landed on Wilkes Island and the southern shore of Wake Island. Soon 1,000 men of the Naval Special Landing Force were ashore. The 100-man detachment that hit Wilkes Island was met by the marines with rifles and hand grenades, and in a four-hour fight, almost all the Japanese were killed.

From his command post Commander Cunningham, the naval commander, sent a message to Pearl Harbor: "Enemy Apparently Landing."

The marine five-inch guns would not bear on the landing craft so they were of no use. The marines put together some other guns, a three-inch boat gun and machine guns. They knocked out several of the landing barges but most of the troops got ashore. They fanned out across the atoll, being stopped when they encountered the knots of defending marines.

At 4:30 that morning Commander Cunningham sent another message: "The enemy is on the island. The issue is in doubt." By 5 o'clock there were 1,500 Japanese ashore on Wake and about 80 marines left to fight them. All the rest of the defenders were on Peale or on Wilkes Island.

The Japanese reached Camp One and invaded the hospital. They were stopped by about 40 marines on a defense line that crossed the airfield. Then the Japanese dive bombers came in again and attacked all the positions. The marines could now count about 20 ships offshore. All were Japanese.

Marine communications began to break down. But the marines did have one bit of news, very bad news. From Pearl Harbor came a message stating that there would be no American ships in the vicinity of Wake Island in the next 24 hours. Fletcher was still fueling.

By 5 A.M. the Japanese had secured a firm beachhead and were gradually expanding it. Only on Wilkes Island had the marines triumphed over the Japanese and killed all but one of the enemy. He escaped only by playing dead. But on the other two islands the Japanese were steadily making gains.

The great difference between Admiral Kimmel, who had made the plan for the relief of Wake Island, and Admiral Pye, who succeeded him in temporary command of the Pacific Fleet, was that one was a fighting man and one was not.

In his history of U. S. naval operations in World War II, Samuel Eliot Morison alluded to this difference, although he did not write about it directly. Kimmel, he wrote, was inclined to decide what the enemy would do and then act accordingly. Pye could also estimate what the enemy might do, but would not act until the enemy had done it.

Until the Pearl Harbor raid, Admiral Pye had been commander of the Battleship Force. But the Japanese shot his force out from under him and so he was without a command until President Roosevelt ordered the removal of Admiral Kimmel and placed Pye in temporary command.

Pye was very uncomfortable with the responsibility of the fleet thrust on his shoulders. By the time he took command, fleet intelligence knew, from papers found in a wrecked Japanese plane, that there had been six carriers involved in the Pearl Harbor raid. Where were they now? Pye wondered, but not for long. From radio intercepts the fleet soon knew that two of the Japanese carriers had left the formation and gone to Wake. All the more reason, then, for the American fleet to seek the battle Admiral Kimmel had put in motion. But even Pye was not basically at fault for the failure to do so. After he had ordered Admiral Brown to turn north and support the Wake Island relief expedition, Admiral Pye was in touch with Admiral Stark, who was just being relieved as Chief of Naval Operations. Admiral Stark said that in Washington they were thinking that Wake Island was a liability, and he authorized Pye to evacuate the forces there rather than strengthen them.

So at the highest level, the navy had decided not to fight at Wake. That attitude was more of the same sort of thinking that had caused the surprise at Pearl Harbor. It was not then apparent to Washington that if the United States was going to win the struggle against Japan, a new navy had to come into being.

This new navy was epitomized by Admiral Chester W.

Nimitz, the new commander of the Pacific Fleet. Had he been at Pearl Harbor when the relief expedition went off, the battle would have been fought and quite probably won. But it took a man with a more aggressive spirit than Admiral Pye to order a fight when Washington did not want it.

On December 21 and 22 when Admiral Fletcher was fueling and moving away from Wake rather than toward it, Admiral Pye sent him several conflicting dispatches.

1. The *Saratoga* was to move up to within 200 miles of Wake and send a strike force to find and attack the Japanese.
   That order was sent and then countermanded.
2. The seaplane tender *Tangier* was to be sent ahead to Wake to evacuate the civilians on the atoll.
   That order was sent and then countermanded.

The irresolution at Pearl Harbor was matched by that of Admiral Fletcher. He did nothing but continue to fuel.

By December 22 fleet intelligence estimated that two Japanese carriers, two battleships, and two heavy cruisers were near Wake. Admiral Pye became very nervous. What would happen to the *Saratoga*? If she were sunk or damaged, he thought, the enemy might come back and attack Pearl Harbor again. Or worse, the Japanese might come from Wake and land on the Hawaiian Islands. Being a battleship man, Admiral Pye worried about risking a carrier against battleships. Here, indeed, was the old naval thinking at work, still controlling American strategy in the new era of the aircraft carrier. And to make it worse, all Pye's fears were confirmed by his chief of staff, Admiral Milo F. Draemel, who was also a battleship man.

Early on December 22 (December 23 Wake time) the dispatch from Commander Cunningham announcing the landing of the Japanese on Wake arrived at Pearl Harbor. It was brought to Pye by Captain C. H. McMorris, who was now operations officer of the fleet. McMorris, Pye, and Draemel began to discuss what to do, and they were still discussing it at 7:30 in the morning when the second dispatch from Wake came in: "Enemy on island—issue in doubt."

The three decided it was too late to evacuate or to relieve Wake. But what about the naval battle that Admiral Kimmel had sought? It lay right there before them. Fletcher's force could engage immediately and Brown's task force could move shortly thereafter. Admiral Halsey's task force was near enough to get into the action, too. And the United States desperately needed a victory at this point. A fighting admiral would have ordered Fletcher into action.

But in view of the weakened nature of the Pacific Fleet in the loss of the battleships, could the battle be justified? Admiral Pye decided not, and thus lost his one chance for greatness. Had he not been a battleship man he would have realized (as the navy later did), that the battleship fleet had been more of a liability than an asset. The existing battleships were all too slow to keep up with carriers and cruisers, and the proof of their impotence would be shown in the next three years, when they were never used for anything but bombardment support of amphibious invasions.

So at 9:11 on December 22 Admiral Pye ordered Fletcher and Brown to turn away from battle and return to Pearl Harbor. Aboard the *Saratoga* the order was greeted with dismay, and Fletcher's staff tried to press him to disregard it and go on into battle. The talk was so mutinous that Admiral Fitch retired from the bridge, mostly because he felt the same way. Fletcher, however, was much relieved and lost no time in turning and moving away.

On Wake the fighting was continuing. When Commander Cunningham received the message that no friendly ships could be expected within 24 hours, he knew that the relief expedition had been called back. When Major Devereux told him that organized resistance could not last much longer and asked about relief, Cunningham had to say there would be none. So at about 7:30 on the morning of December 23, Commander Cunningham told Major Devereux that the time had come to surrender.

Commander Cunningham and Major Devereux then arranged the surrender (unconditional). Then Major Devereux had to visit all the marine outposts to tell the men to lay down their arms, and fighting continued for several hours until he could do so.

Nearly 500 men of the army, navy, and marine corps and nearly 1,200 civilians became prisoners of war.

The Japanese took possession of Wake Island that afternoon and renamed it Otori Shima, or Bird Island.

So on the American perimeter by Christmas 1941, Guam was lost to the Japanese and now Wake was lost, too. What remained were the Philippines, under siege but hopeful of relief from the American mainland, Hawaii, Midway, the Aleutians, the Panama Canal Zone, and American Samoa. The Japanese had their eyes on all these places, either for invasion or for attack.

CHAPTER FOUR

Against Sabotage and Espionage

In Hawaii, after the army declared martial law, the command began to talk about evacuation of all the Japanese in the islands, either to concentrate them on one island or to move them to the mainland. The reason was the same as that which had prompted martial law: the army fear of sabotage and espionage, and the need to strengthen the defenses of Hawaii against possible invasion attempts by the Japanese.

For several years the military and the Federal Bureau of Investigation had compiled lists of aliens who might be supposed to be disloyal in wartime. But in the summer of 1941 the army had declared that if the Japanese remained loyal to the United States in a war with Japan, they would be fairly treated. Now that war had come, there had been no sabotage and no espionage except by the members of the Japanese consulate. There was only one incident of disloyalty and that Nisei was dead. Lieutenant General Delos C. Emmons, who replaced General Short in command in Hawaii, renewed this pledge on December 21. However, two days before that in Washington, Navy Secretary Frank Knox persuaded the Roosevelt cabinet that all Japanese in Hawaii should be moved to islands other than Oahu. On January 10 the War Department asked Emmons if this was practicable.

The general replied that such a move would be dangerous and destructive to the islands' economy and to the defenses of Oahu since most of the skilled employees who worked for the navy and army were Japanese. At a time when Hawaii had about half the troops it needed, this move would require many more troops to guard the island. If they were going to move the Japanese, said the general, they should move them to the mainland. In that case they would have to import other workers by the thousands to replace them since the Japanese population of Hawaii was 118,000, of which 20,000 were Japanese citizens and 98,000 American citizens.

For weeks the army and Washington hemmed and hawed about the Japanese in Hawaii. General Emmons did not trust them, but when Washington ordered that the army discharge all Japanese labor who worked for the army, he suddenly realized that this would paralyze the army. Washington quickly backed down and rescinded the order.

In Washington President Roosevelt was pressing for the evacuation of the Japanese and was not concerned with their civil liberties. All that, he said, was taken care of by his own executive orders and martial law. Nobody on Hawaii had any rights anymore. This was war. The government could do as it pleased!

The matter was taken up by the Roosevelt cabinet again, and Secretary Knox again urged evacuation. When the army said the evacuation should be to the mainland, President Roosevelt was stunned. He wanted the Japanese concentrated on Molokai Island in a concentration camp, guarded by the army.

The Joint Chiefs of Staff recommended that the 20,000 Japanese citizens be evacuated to the mainland as dangerous aliens. And that is where the matter was left in March 1942. In the meantime, the army was ridding itself of some of its hysteria and in March was disinclined to pursue this matter further. The army estimate of "dangerous aliens" had dropped to 1,500. When Assistant Secretary of War John J. McCloy visited Hawaii he learned that both army and navy commands there had now decided that the way to treat the Japanese was "as citizens of an occupied country." That, of course, is how all the people of the islands were being treated under martial law.

President Roosevelt and Secretary Knox continued to press for evacuation of the Japanese, and the army continued to stall. The matter remained on the table for months. Ultimately fewer than 2,000 "dangerous" Japanese were evacuated to the mainland before the matter died down in 1943.

But the distrust of the Japanese continued on the mainland, where they were sent to concentration camps as a part of the American defense, and in Hawaii.

For more than a year the protection of Hawaii had been shared by the 298th and 299th Infantry Regiments of the National Guard, which had been called to federal service in 1940. Many of the enlisted men and some officers were of Japanese descent. In May 1942, when new American troops began to arrive in the islands, General Emmons took all the Japanese from these National Guard units, organized them into a Provisional Battalion, and sent them to the mainland. Thus was formed the 100th Infantry Battalion, which landed on the Salerno Beachhead in Italy in September 1943 and later became part of the 442nd Regimental Combat Team, a Nisei organization that became the most decorated for valor of any in the army of the United States.

In spite of the loyalty shown by the Japanese in Hawaii and on the mainland, the federal government, from President Roosevelt on down, was determined to persecute the Japanese and did. But this was just a part of the defense program. General Short had urgently requested reinforcement of the Hawaii garrison before he was relieved, and by December 13, 1941, two fast transports were loaded with 7,000 men, fighter planes, bombs, and ammunition, and were ready to leave San Francisco for Hawaii. But the navy refused to let them go without an escort, so they waited and did not reach Hawaii until two weeks after the attack. Then a second convoy of 11 ships left San Francisco and arrived in Hawaii on January 7. These convoys brought 15,000 troops to Hawaii, raising the garrison to more than 58,000. Antiaircraft guns, ammunition, and fighter planes and bombers came in, and by the second week of January, the Hawaii military authorities felt fairly secure against the possibility of invasion.

The problem of defense of the islands other than Oahu remained. General Emmons pointed out that it might be possible for the Japanese to land on one of the other islands or several of them and thus starve out the Oahu garrison. Responding to these arguments, the War Department changed its policy and allowed the defense of the outer islands, particularly after the Twenty-seventh Division arrived in the spring. So a garrison was approved of 74,000 troops on Oahu, 13,000 on Hawaii, and about 13,000 distributed among the five other inhabited islands.

The Japanese made another attack on Hawaii on March 4, 1942. Two Japanese Kawanishi flying boats came from the Marshall Islands to refuel from submarines at French Frigate Shoals and then flew to Oahu, 500 miles to the southeast. Army radar spotted the planes about 90 miles off Kauai, and four fighters were sent after them but did not find them. One Japanese plane skirted the coast of Oahu. The other flew up to the north shore, and in the middle of the night dropped four 500-pound bombs that landed in the woods on the slopes of Mount Tantalus, about two miles from downtown Honolulu. The bombs did no damage except to break a few windows. The Japanese were toying with the idea of invading Hawaii and planned more such flights for intelligence purposes, but when the U. S. Navy deduced that the planes had refueled at French Frigate Shoals, they sent ships up there to keep a permanent watch and deny the protected water to Japanese submarines. So next time the submarines appeared they found their fueling place occupied, and went away.

By the spring of 1942, then, the Hawaii outpost of the American perimeter was secure. The air raid warning system had been perfected. The bombers and fighters destroyed by the Japanese in 1941 had been replaced and augmented. Troops were dug in all around the islands and were prepared for fighting if the Japanese should appear. An inspection team from Washington came through in April 1942 and declared that morale was high and the army in Hawaii was prepared for war.

CHAPTER FIVE

West Coast Defense

Until the attack on Pearl Harbor Americans had long felt that the Pacific Ocean was their best defense against attack, but suddenly on December 7, 1941, it seemed that all the defenses had evaporated and the West Coast lay open to Japanese attack and maybe invasion.

The major army concern was the defense industries up and down the coast, from California to Washington State. In December 1941 half the military aircraft produced in the United States were coming from eight plants in the Los Angeles area. Add to that the Boeing Factories in Washington and the shipyards in California, Oregon, and Washington, and the concerns grew broad indeed. These fears were fanned in the first two weeks after Pearl Harbor by rumors and reports of Japanese carrier forces steaming toward the United States.

So the War Department established the Western Defense Command on December 11 and concentrated on reinforcing the ground and air garrisons along the West Coast. By the end of the year 1941 the West Coast defenses included six infantry divisions, a brigade of cavalry, 14 antiaircraft regiments, three fighter groups, and three bombardment groups of aircraft. The ground strength numbered about 250,000 men.

Pearl Harbor brought the fear of imminent attack to the West Coast, but by the end of December it had subsided. The threat was perceived as coming from the air, and so air defenses became the matter of primary importance.

The only real Japanese activity along the Pacific Coast in those first months of war was by submarines. The Japanese Sixth Fleet, the submarine command, had ordered nine I-boats to the West Coast to attack shipping and disrupt communications. Seven of them carried patrol planes. The submarines arrived off the West Coast about December 17, and were dispersed from Cape Flattery in the north to San Diego. They sank two tankers and damaged one freighter. The Japanese planned to shell coastal installations on Christmas Eve, 1941, but the plans were changed and the I-boats were ordered to return to Kwajalein.

Two more Japanese submarines came to the West Coast in February 1942. The first to arrive was the *I-8*, which patrolled north from San Francisco to the Washington coast without seeing any ships and then returned to Japan. The second was the *I-17*, which arrived off San Diego on February 19. On February 23 the *I-17* surfaced near Santa Barbara and shot 13 rounds of 5.5-inch ammunition at some oil installations. No material damage was done.

But the attack may have had a psychological impact in helping trigger what was called the battle of Los Angeles.

For more than a month some of the people of Los Angeles had been carrying on a noisy campaign, calling for the removal of the resident Japanese population. By the night of February 24, the level of tension was very high. The military were expecting disorder and riots. At two o'clock in the morning a series of reports of suspicious activities came in. One of them said that coastal radar had picked up an unidentified aircraft coming in from the ocean toward Los Angeles. Blackout was ordered and antiaircraft guns were trained at the sky. The guns began to fire an hour later. The first victim was a meteorological balloon flying over Santa Monica. In the next hour the guns fired 1,400 rounds of three-inch ammunition against various "targets." Two days of investigation produced only conflicting reports. The army concluded that perhaps five unidentified aircraft had flown over the area. The navy concluded that it had all been hot air. The report might have been started by the plane of the *I-17*, but that submarine was soon sailing north where it claimed two ships off Cape Mendocino before returning to Japan. So the battle of Los Angeles ended and the authorities realized that much work was needed on the antiaircraft defenses before they began to make any sense.

But the most extensive action for the defense of the West Coast was taken in the imprisonment of the entire West Coast Japanese population, citizens and non-citizens, in the most disgraceful violations of civil liberties since the Palmer raids of the 1920s.

The census of 1940 showed that 112,000 Japanese and Japanese-Americans were living in the three West Coast states, 41,000 of them Japanese citizens, the rest Americans. The Pearl Harbor raids triggered an immediate public outcry against the Japanese in America. This was to be expected because such racism had existed since the building of the Pacific Railroad.

On December 10 an agent of the Treasury Department reported to army authorities that 20,000 Japanese in San Francisco were about to rise up against the government. Without checking, the Ninth Corps Area staff started action to arrest the Japanese. The plan was immediately approved by the corps commander. The next morning the army called the local FBI agent in charge, who laughed at the report as the wild imaginings of a discharged FBI agent. The plan was stopped but the corps commander reported the event to Washington in a manner that seemed to authenticate the danger. And so the ball began to roll.

By February the federal authorities were registering all enemy aliens. The wildest rumors were coursing through Washington, passed along by persons in authority. The Army Provost Marshal declared "that not a single ship had sailed from our Pacific ports without being subsequently attacked." The truth was that not a ship sailed from the Pacific coast ports that *was* attacked.

However, the hysteria was building and the appearance of the two Japanese submarines in February added enormously to the buildup. But the army could not escape responsibility. A GHQ intelligence bulletin of January 21 concluded that an espionage ring of Japanese and Japanese-Americans existed and was working underground. There were no facts and no proof, just allegations, but they fanned the fires. The fact that there had been no sabotage or incidents of espionage was regarded by the army authorities as "ominous."

The publication of the Roberts report on the Pearl Harbor attack late in January fanned the flames even more. A special investigating commission, the Roberts Commission, stated that there had been widespread espionage in Hawaii by the Japanese consular staff (true), and by residents (false). But the false charges rang as loudly as the true, until after the war when the Roberts report was proved to be false. In January 1942 it was regarded as gospel.

By mid-February 1942 the federal authorities had arrested about 1,300 Japanese as "dangerous." But then the West Coast members of Congress acted. They organized a caucus of congressmen and senators, which demanded action to protect the homes of Americans. (This did not include Japanese-Americans.)

The plans were made for the arrest and internment of the Japanese, and they were referred to President Roosevelt, who approved them in the second week of February. The congressional caucus approved wholeheartedly of arresting all Japanese in Oregon, Washington, and California, and so a War Relocation Authority was established and Milton S. Eisenhower took charge of the treatment of the Japanese. The evacuation began in March.

Meanwhile the Canadians in British Columbia were doing the same, even more quickly. They moved 21,000 Japanese, mostly Canadian citizens, out of the western provinces and to the interior where they were imprisoned in camps. In Alaska the entire Japanese population of 230 people was interned. And throughout 1942 the Japanese-Americans were moved, many of them to the concentration camps on the Colorado River of the desert. It was all justified in the name of national defense. Only nearly 50 years later did the Japanese begin to get compensation, and that was small recompense for property they had been forced to sacrifice and the misery that the American hysteria of 1942 had brought.

CHAPTER SIX

The Decision

In the spring of 1942 the Japanese juggernaut was moving along rapidly in the South Pacific, but Admiral Yamamoto was nervous about the future, as long as the American Pacific Fleet remained in being. He knew that it was only a question of time before the Americans more than replaced the battleships put out of action in the Pearl Harbor attack. He was very much concerned lest Americans attack the Japanese. Enough material had already appeared in the world press about the building of the new B-29 Superfortresses, and defense officials had unguardedly indicated that these were being built for attack on Japan.

And if such attacks were to come, where would they come from? One logical place was Midway Island, the American forward base in the Central Pacific. Another possible point of departure was Alaska, and particularly the Aleutian Islands, which jut out almost to reach Siberia in the North Pacific. From the Aleutians to Japan it is 2,000 miles, within the range of the Superfortresses. Further, the Aleutians might be used as the Japanese used Hitokappa Bay for the assault on Hawaii, as a takeoff point for task forces to raid Japan.

The Japanese Imperial Army was talking about extending the frontiers of empire to New Guinea, Samoa, and Fiji. That was all very well, but Yamamoto was thinking along different lines, of the need to protect the Japanese home islands and the need to deal with the American Pacific Fleet. So while the army planners were talking about New Guinea, Yamamoto was thinking about Midway and the Aleutians, to deal with several problems:

1. Denying the Americans of a Central Pacific base of operations.

2. Luring the American fleet to destruction.

3. Possibly capturing the Hawaiian Islands in the future.

4. Establishing a base of operations in the Aleutian Islands that could be used to keep the Eastern Pacific under control and deny the Americans the chance to send bombing planes across the north to raid Japan.

Out of this thinking came a three-part operational plan that Yamamoto proposed to the naval high command. Five major forces would cooperate to carry out this master plan.

First, three groups of submarines would be sent out, one group to watch the Hawaiian Islands, one group to watch the Aleutians and Alaska, and one group to watch Midway. Second, the carrier striking force, which had raided Hawaii in 1941, would now carry the battle to Midway. Third, an occupation force for Midway would be led by Admiral Kondo, the chief of the Second Fleet, and it would carry the troops who would land on Midway and take possession. Fourth, the main body of the fleet would be under the command of Yamamoto himself and include the three newest battleships and a light carrier, and the Aleutians screen force, which would consist of four battleships and two light cruisers. Fifth, the Aleutians force under Admiral Boshiro Hosogaya would include two carriers, three cruisers, and transports carrying the occupation forces who would take over the islands of Adak, Attu, and Kiska.

The campaign in the Aleutians would open with Admiral Hosogaya's two carriers delivering a powerful bombardment on Dutch Harbor, Alaska, on June 3. This bombing would confuse the Americans at Pearl Harbor and prepare the way for the occupation of the Aleutians. The Aleutian force would then be waiting, halfway between the Japanese main body and the Aleutians, prepared to intercept any American naval units that came from Hawaii or from the mainland United States. What Yamamoto expected was that the bombing of Dutch Harbor would cause the Pacific Fleet to move toward Alaska, thus getting it out of the way for the occupation of Midway, to return to be dealt with by the carrier striking force and the main body of the Japanese fleet at leisure.

The Yamamoto plan was sent up to Tokyo that spring, where it met a very mixed reaction. The senior naval staff did not like it, for it placed their fleet in jeopardy far from Japanese waters. But Yamamoto, as in the planning of the Pearl Harbor attack, was insistent and again threatened that if his plan was not accepted he would resign as chief of the Combined Fleet. Because the Pearl Harbor plan had been so great a success (in the eyes of the naval authorities, not Yamamoto) and because of his insistence, it was not turned down. Then, in mid-April, when the bombers of Lieutenant Colonel Jimmy Doolittle's force raided Japan, the Yamamoto plan for Midway became far more acceptable to the naval authorities. As Yamamoto said, it was absolutely necessary to deal with the Pacific Fleet soon, and to take precautions against the bombing of Japan. This plan did both. So before the battle of the Coral Sea, the Midway–Aleutians operation was scheduled by the Japanese.

CHAPTER SEVEN

Striking the American Perimeter in the South

On March 17, 1942, after agreements between President Roosevelt and Prime Minister Winston Churchill of Britain, the United States assumed responsibility for the defense of the entire Pacific Ocean, including New Zealand and Australia, which thus became new parts of the American perimeter.

Since the two leaders had agreed that Hitler must be defeated before Japan could be dealt with, this assumption of responsibility indicated that the United States would conduct a strategic defensive program. But it was also understood that the protection of lines of communication in the Pacific must have a high priority, and when these were threatened strong action would have to be taken.

Since Japan had achieved its first set of objectives in the Pacific in about three months, half the time that had been allocated, Imperial General Headquarters looked around for new worlds to conquer. They soon became afflicted with what some wiser Japanese heads termed "the victory disease." They began to believe their own propaganda, which held that one Japanese soldier was the equivalent of three soldiers of any other nation and perhaps more when compared to the soldiers of the Western world, for whom the Japanese had developed supreme contempt. So plans were made for further expansion to the south by the Imperial Army, even as Admiral Yamamoto was planning expansion eastward across the Pacific, to Midway, Hawaii, and the Aleutian Islands.

Up until May 1, 1942, the Japanese had lost only 23 naval vessels, none of them larger than a destroyer; 67 merchant ships; a few hundred aircraft, and a few thousand soldiers and sailors. This was much less than the 30 percent loss that had been anticipated, and persuaded the young officers who actually made the war plans that they could safely expand their original horizons and make reality of what had been only dreams.

In the south this included the Solomons and Papua New Guinea, next to Australia. Then the next step would be to New Caledonia, Fiji, and Samoa to cut the lines of communication between the United States and Australia–New Zealand. In the east it included Midway and the Aleutians, and then Hawaii. All of these conquests had been indicated in the Japanese basic war plan of 1938. The difference was that now the Imperial General Headquarters was prepared to try to carry it out ahead of schedule.

In addition to this plan, which was basically the army's, Admiral Yamamoto, the commander of the Combined Fleet, was ridden by the need to deal with the American Pacific Fleet as soon as possible. Once that was done, the Japanese fleet would be masters of the Pacific and could sail anywhere. If that was not done, he knew, the Americans would steadily gain power until they would choose the scene and conditions of battle, and if that happened, all would be lost because Yamamoto knew that in a battle of attrition Japan did not have the staying power to match the United States.

So while the army planned for the capture of new territories that would include American Samoa, Admiral Yamamoto devoted his efforts to the Eastern Pacific and the destruction of the American perimeter there. The two plans were put into motion almost simultaneously in Tokyo in the spring of 1942. First, the navy would protect the army's preliminary movements into the Coral Sea—the capture of a base in the Solomons and the capture of Port Moresby in New Guinea. That would happen in May. Then the Combined Fleet ships sent south to cover those operations would hurry north again to participate in the Midway and Aleutians operations. After that the second phase of the southern operations would be carried out, capturing Noumea, Fiji, and Samoa. Then attention could be turned to Hawaii, and finally to Australia. The American perimeter would be shoved back to the continental United States, and the American presence in the Pacific would be eliminated. Asia and the Pacific would belong to the Greater East Asia Co-Prosperity Sphere.

In May 1942, although the Combined Chiefs of Staff had committed the United States to a defensive posture in the Pacific, Rear Admiral Ernest J. King, the navy chief, felt the new responsibilities of defending the new perimeter that included Australia, and so when Japanese activity was noted in the New Guinea area, he had Admiral Nimitz dispatch two carrier task forces to the Coral Sea region. They were on hand early in May when the Japanese moved to carry out the first phase of their southern expansion: establishment of a seaplane base in the lower Solomons for reconnaissance of Australia and capture of Port Moresby as a stepping stone to Fiji and Samoa. After that the Tulagi force would move on to capture Ocean and Nauru islands, which the Japanese wanted for their resources.

The Japanese landed at Tulagi on May 3 and the American carrier task forces first attacked the Japanese Tulagi force on May 4, crippling the new seaplane base there. The Japanese Port Moresby force set out cautiously for its objectives, but was called back to Rabaul because American task forces were milling about in the Coral Sea. The Japanese protective force, which included the two major carriers *Shokaku* and *Zuikaku*, engaged in the first carrier battle of the Pacific war on May 8, with the result that the American carrier *Lexington* was lost and the carrier *Yorktown* damaged, but the *Shokaku* was also damaged and the *Zuikaku* lost most of her aircraft and pilots. With this result, although the Japanese claimed a victory, they decided to postpone the Port Moresby invasion. They might need more naval support, and they would not be able to get it from the Combined Fleet until after the Midway and Aleutians operations had been carried out.

So the first foray of the Japanese against the new American perimeter had resulted in failure, but from the Japanese point of view not irretrievable failure but simply delay.

CHAPTER EIGHT

First Midway,
Then Hawaii

When those two Japanese Kawanishi flying boats had
raided Oahu on the night of March 3, 1942, Admiral Nimitz
had suspected that the Japanese were keeping an eye on
Hawaii for some reason, and the reason had to be the pros-
pect of invasion of the islands. His concern was amplified
a week later when another of these long-range four-engined
Kawanishis was shot down by four Marine Corps fighters
off Midway.

Obviously, the Japanese had more plans for attack on the
American perimeter.

That was March. In April the radio intercepts and the
breaking of the Japanese naval codes had given information
that enabled Nimitz to send his two carrier forces down to
the South Pacific to stop the development of the Solomons
and the Japanese capture of Port Moresby. But even as the
battle of the Coral Sea was developing, Nimitz had more
clues to something much more important that was coming
in the Central Pacific. What was it going to be? Another
raid on Hawaii? An attempt to invade Hawaii? An assault
on the American mainland? An assault on Midway? An
invasion of Alaska or the Aleutians? It could be any one of
these.

In fact, the younger staff officers of the Combined Fleet
ambitiously proposed invading Hawaii, but the army objected. It was too fully occupied in China and the South
Pacific, the army said, to spare the personnel. If the Amer-

61

icans had 100,000 men to defend the Hawaiian Islands, the Japanese would have to have at least that many to attack. (Based on their previous experiences the Japanese totally underestimated the needs of an invasion force, which the Americans had found to be at least three times as many invaders as defenders.) Even if it was true, as the young planners indicated, that the large population of Japanese and Japanese-Americans could be expected to be at least docile, if not enthusiastic, the drain on manpower was still too great. Later, said Imperial General Headquarters.

Since one of the major reasons for the whole program was Admiral Yamamoto's conviction that he had to deal with the U. S. Pacific Fleet soon, the plan was then whittled down. It would be Midway. And after Midway was taken and the base built up, then the navy and army could talk about Hawaii.

Midway was what Admiral Nagumo, the victor of Pearl Harbor, called "the sentinel of Hawaii." It is one of the Hawaiian chain, the farthest occupied island to the west, a sandy atoll consisting of two islands, Sand Island and Eastern Island. A barrier reef encloses both islands.

Midway had already come to Japanese attention on the night of December 7, 1941. After the main Japanese force had struck Hawaii that night an independent unit of two destroyers had bombarded the island causing 14 casualties, burning the seaplane hangar, and destroying one the American PBY patrol planes stationed on the island.

As a part of the reinforcement of Hawaii after the Pearl Harbor attack, Midway was also reinforced by the Americans with bombers and fighter plane squadrons. After that the Japanese sent submarines to the atoll to bombard, but the shore guns and the aircraft attacked them and in each case forced the I-boats to abandon their efforts.

So in the spring of 1942, as the Americans changed and reinforced their perimeter, sacrificing Guam, Wake, and the Philippines, but extending it in the Southwest Pacific, the Japanese were doing the same. They wanted Midway, Hawaii, and the Aleutian Islands as their eastern perimeter, keeping the Americans at bay. The Doolittle raid of mid-April, which came after their basic plans had been laid, simply reinforced the feeling of need and helped convince the Naval General Staff that this whole operation was essential. Some of the senior officers believed that the Doolittle planes had flown from Midway.

The result of all these operations would be a perimeter that extended from Kiska, to Midway, to Wake Island, to the Marshall Islands, to the Gilberts, to Guadalcanal and Port Moresby. With these sentinel posts they should be able to prevent any more raids on the home islands and to deal with the submarine threat that now came from Hawaii by way of Midway.

There would be no attack on Hawaii until after Midway was occupied and the American fleet defeated. Then French Frigate Shoals would be occupied and several raids might be made on Hawaii, too. After the occupation, raiders from Midway would have no difficulty in reaching Hawaii when they wished.

Suspecting that the Japanese target would be Midway, Admiral Nimitz flew there early in May to inspect the defenses. Marine Lieutenant Colonel Harold Shannon was in charge of the ground troops, and when Nimitz asked him if he could hold the island against a Japanese amphibious assault, he said he could.

The marines had antiboat guns and antiaircraft guns, but they got more. Two companies of the new Second Marine Raider Batallion were sent to the island. A 37-mm antiaircraft battery was added. Bombproof dugouts were built. More dive bombers and more marine fighters were brought in. More antiaircraft guns and five light tanks, 18 B-17 bombers, and four B-26 bombers were taken to Midway. Ten motor torpedo boats were added.

The defenses then consisted of 121 aircraft and 3,000 officers and men to defend the atoll.

By May 10, two days after the battle of the Coral Sea, the Japanese plans for the triple operation of occupying Midway, occupying the Aleutians, and defeating the American Pacific Fleet were being translated into orders, and these orders were broadcast, so that Admiral Nimitz began to get an idea of what the Japanese were up to. Surprisingly the first effort would be an air raid in Alaskan waters, which was supposed to confuse Admiral Nimitz. Before he could emerge from the confusion, Midway would be occupied by Japanese troops, as would the Aleutians, and when he brought out the Pacific Fleet, the Japanese Combined Fleet with all its power would be there to destroy the Americans.

On May 15 Admiral King predicted that in nine days the Midway expeditionary force would depart from Guam. Naval intelligence in Washington had another idea; the whole Midway plan was a giant hoax to mask a new raid on Pearl Harbor. But Nimitz believed his own radio intelligence team, and so that day he issued orders for every ship in the Pacific Fleet that had been in the South Pacific to hurry back to Pearl Harbor.

What did Nimitz have to work with? He had a limited number of ships, and he still had to send escorts with convoys to Australia. Also, he knew that the Japanese were planning something in the Aleutians. What was he to do about that? Could he send any ships? On May 17 he decided to form the North Pacific Force with two heavy cruisers, three light cruisers, and ten destroyers. That was all he could spare.

The carrier *Saratoga* had been torpedoed by a Japanese submarine that spring, but was now repaired and at San Diego training her air group; she would not be able to take part.

The *Lexington* was sunk. The *Yorktown* was damaged. The *Enterprise* and the *Hornet*, under Admiral Halsey's command, had been rushed down to the South Pacific for the Coral Sea battle but had arrived too late. They were ordered back. The *Yorktown,* damaged by bombs, came back on May 27. In two days the Pearl Harbor navy yard had made her shipshape again, using 1,400 men and working 24 hours a day.

The *Yorktown* sailed on May 30. Admiral Halsey came home sick, so his task force was turned over to Rear Admiral Raymond Spruance, Nimitz's chief of staff. So Nimitz had three carriers, and he did not know how many the Japanese had—maybe the six that had raided Pearl Harbor. Actually the Japanese would have sent six big carriers, except that the battle of the Coral Sea had deprived them of the service

of two, *Shokaku* and *Zuikaku*, for the next few weeks. So
the Japanese had in their attack force four fleet carriers, two
light carriers scheduled for the Aleutians operation, and one
light carrier that accompanied the battleship fleet commanded by Admiral Yamamoto.

Although the Japanese naval force was much larger and
stronger than the American, Admiral Nimitz had one great
advantage. He knew what his enemy was doing and when,
and the Japanese did not know that the Americans knew,
or that the Americans were moving their forces to Midway
before the Japanese got there. Yamamoto expected the
American naval force to be still at Pearl Harbor until the
attack on Midway would bring them out to be destroyed.
So the three American carriers sailed, accompanied by all
the cruisers and destroyers available. There was not a single
battleship. The new battleships were not yet ready for battle,
and the old battleships of the fleet had been sent to San
Francisco because Admiral King was nervous about an invasion attempt against the mainland. Besides, they could
not keep up with the carriers and would have been a liability.

Nimitz told his commanders to go northeast of Midway
and wait there beyond the search range of the enemy. He
anticipated that the 700-mile searches by the Midway-based
aircraft would locate the Japanese carriers, and that the
American carriers' presence would not be suspected.

The Japanese movement toward Midway began early in
May with the dispatch of several submarines. Two of them
went to French Frigate Shoals, expecting to find Japanese
flying boats there and to service them, but instead they saw
an American seaplane tender at anchor, and they quickly
departed. The main force of submarines on June 3 formed
a scout line between Oahu and Midway and waited for the
Pacific Fleet to come out, not knowing that the fleet force
had already departed from Pearl Harbor days before the
submarines arrived. So, unlike the Pearl Harbor attack, the
surprise element was all on the side of the Americans.

The first group of surface ships to move out from Japan
was Admiral Kakuta's Second Mobile Force, headed for
the Aleutians. Admiral Nagumo's carrier striking force,
which had the dual jobs of striking Midway and then finding

and destroying the American carrier fleet, left the Inland Sea on May 26. Admiral Yamamoto followed two days later with the main body of the Combined Fleet, including the battleship *Yamato* with her 18-inch guns and the other battleships with their 16-inch guns.

The Japanese were happy and confident of victory, except Admiral Nagumo, who as usual was worried. He did not feel that he had been given enough time after the last raid, on the Indian Ocean, from which his ships had just returned to Japan on April 23.

Admiral Nagumo's task was first to attack Midway and destroy the American air power there on June 4. The landings would be made on June 5. As the Japanese steamed across the Pacific, the defenders of Midway were busy, building underwater obstacles and stringing barbed wire along the beaches, mining the approaches and the beaches. The airmen in the B-17s and the PBYs ran air searches every day. Twenty-two Catalinas searched out 700 miles. But as the Japanese carrier force approached Midway it was hidden by cloud cover. The clouds were so thick on June 2 that Admiral Nagumo lost contact with his ships and had to break radio silence to order his ships to change course.

The 25 American submarines available were also out, 19 of them searching and covering the American Midway force, and six of them moving toward the Aleutians.

The American carriers and their task forces fueled on May 31 and June 1 and then moved to a point about 325 miles northeast of Midway. The carriers were now outside the range of land-based air search, so they flew their own antisubmarine and combat air patrol and search missions 150 miles out, but the enemy was not there.

On June 3, just before 9 o'clock in the morning, an American PBY at the end of its 700-mile search plan spotted 11 ships. The PBY crew tracked the ships for several hours and reported. This was a part of the transport group of the Midway Occupation Force.

When the news reached Midway, the commander of the island sent out nine B-17 bombers that discovered the transports almost 600 miles out and made three high-level attacks. The pilots reported hitting several ships, but actually they did not hit any.

Then four PBYs armed with torpedoes attacked in the moonlight, and one of them torpedoed the oiler *Akebono Maru*. The explosion killed several men and slowed the ship, but she remained with the formation.

On that evening of June 3, the American carriers were 300 miles northeast of Midway, about 400 miles away from Admiral Nagumo's carriers. The Americans changed course that night and steamed toward where they thought the Japanese carriers would be the next morning. The Japanese still did not know that the Americans were anywhere in the vicinity.

At 4:30 on the morning of June 4, the *Yorktown* launched 10 dive bombers to cover a semicircle to the north, out 100 miles just so the American force would not be surprised by the enemy. The Japanese were then about 200 miles to the west of the Americans, just launching their first strike against Midway Island. A few minutes later American search planes from Midway announced the presence of the Japanese carriers. The message was also intercepted by the American carriers, so they knew where the Japanese were. The Japanese still believed the American carriers were at Pearl Harbor.

Admiral Fletcher was as conservative as always, and he wanted to wait to recover his search planes before he did anything more. As senior officer and commander, he ordered Admiral Spruance to take the *Hornet* and the *Enterprise* southwest and attack the enemy carriers when they found them. He said he would follow as soon as he had recovered his search planes.

The Japanese carrier planes that took off from their carriers at 4:30 headed for Midway, 108 planes, torpedo bombers armed with 800-kilogram bombs, dive bombers, and Zero fighters. On Midway, the American TBF bombers and the army B-26 bombers were ordered by Admiral Nimitz to go out and attack the Japanese carriers. So they flew off at 6:15 without fighter protection. They found the carriers at 7:15, but the Japanese had their combat air patrol in the air. Several of the American planes were shot down immediately. One TBF dropped a torpedo that was exploded by machine gun fire. Another TBF was hit by antiaircraft fire and crashed on the deck of a carrier but bounced off. Of the six TBFs only one returned to Midway. Only two of the B-26s got back and only one of those could fly again. The army pilots made many claims in the next few days, but the fact was that none of the American planes had hit anything.

Just before 6 A.M. the Japanese planes were picked up by the Midway search radar, when they were about 100 miles out. All the planes that could fly got off the ground. The heavy bombers and PBYs were sent out of the way, and the marine fighters flew out to attack the enemy. At 6:15 they encountered the Japanese planes, flying at 12,000 feet. The Americans climbed to 17,000 feet and swooped down to intercept, but they were outnumbered and so busy fighting off attacking Zeros that they could not go after the bombers.

The Japanese high-altitude bombers struck first from 14,000 feet and were followed by the dive bombers. They destroyed the marine command post and mess hall and damaged the power house on Eastern Island. They destroyed oil tanks on Sand Island and the seaplane hangar, and set several buildings afire, including the hospital. The attack ended just before 7 A.M.

At 7:15 the surviving American fighters began to land on Midway. Of the 36 fighters, 17 were missing and seven others were damaged. But the fighter survivors and the antiaircraft gunners claimed about 35 Japanese shot down.

The Japanese leader of the Midway attack group radioed back to the carrier flagship that another strike on Midway was needed. At that time, the decks of the carriers were loaded with 93 planes armed with torpedoes and armor-piercing bombs for use against ships. But search planes sent out to see if there were any American ships about found nothing, and actually Admiral Nagumo did not expect to find anything. The Japanese still thought the American fleet was at Pearl Harbor.

So when the attack leader's message came through, Admiral Nagumo ordered the Japanese planes on the decks to rearm with high-explosive bombs to strike Midway again.

About 15 minutes later a cruiser scout plane reported sighting 10 surface ships—the pilot did not identify the types—about 240 miles from Midway. Admiral Nagumo was not concerned. He could take care of these ships in plenty of time.

But he had second thoughts and a few minutes later ordered his planes to go back to the original scheme and attack the ships. He also demanded from the scout plane pilot a fuller report, and then learned that the ships were cruisers and destroyers, accompanied by a carrier.

So at 8:20 in the morning Admiral Nagumo learned that an American carrier was in the vicinity. What was he to do? The planes that should be attacking the ships had been taken back down to the hangar deck for rearming instead of being sent off. He now had to keep the decks clear to take on the planes from the Midway strike force.

While the admiral was worrying over this problem, the Japanese carriers were beating off attacks by the Midway-based bombers. The dive bombers arrived next. They were not very well-trained pilots and they were not very accurate. No bombs hit the carriers, although one plane strafed a carrier, but only eight of the dive bombers made it back to Midway, and six of those were too badly damaged to fly again.

After the dive bombers, in came 15 B-17 bombers that dropped 127,500 pounds of bombs, and did not hit anything.

Then 11 marine Vindicator bombers came in. They did not hit anything, either, but nine of them got back to Midway.

While the bombers were overhead, underneath the surface the American submarine *Nautilus* came up in the middle of the Japanese formation, fired a torpedo at a battleship, missed, and then dived, to be depth charged intensively, but to survive.

All the action was over by 8:35 that morning. The Japanese carriers were intact; their planes had hit Midway hard and the American riposte had been fended off successfully. The first round of the battle went easily to the Japanese.

The two American carriers of Admiral Spruance's task

force began launching their planes at 7 o'clock in the morning. They were "snooped" by a Japanese reconnaissance plane but the launching was completed. From the carriers *Hornet* and *Enterprise* 116 torpedo bombers, dive bombers, and fighters headed out to find the enemy. Fletcher, as usual, delayed for two hours and then launched his aircraft, but unlike Spruance he only sent off half the available dive bombers.

The four Japanese carriers were moving in a boxlike formation toward Midway, waiting to recover the planes they had sent off on the morning strike against the island. At about 8:30 they began to recover their planes. Then they changed course, and Admiral Nagumo announced that they were soon going to attack the enemy ships.

The dive bombers from the *Hornet* were unable to find the Japanese and flew around until they had to head for Midway to refuel. All the fighters ran out of gas and ditched in the water. But most of the bombers made it to Midway.

The torpedo bombers of the *Hornet* were the first to find the enemy. They had become separated from the dive bombers and the fighters, and so they had no fighter protection. Their leader, Lieutenant Commander John C. Waldron, turned north when they did not immediately sight the Japanese ships where they had been reported to be, and thus soon saw the smoke from the funnels.

As they flew in to attack they were sighted by the Japanese, and antiaircraft fire began to come up from the ships. The Japanese combat air patrol fighters swooped down on the torpedo bombers. One by one the torpedo bombers were shot down as they bored in to the carriers. A few of the planes made it to the point where they could launch torpedoes, but none of the torpedoes hit home. So the attack was a total failure, and only one pilot survived. After his plane was shot down he managed to get out, although his radio operator–gunner did not, and, clinging to a floating seat cushion, he was able to watch the action.

The next attack was made by the 14 torpedo bombers of the *Enterprise*, and 10 of them were shot down. The other four launched their torpedoes, but none of them hit.

The Japanese ships maneuvered to avoid the torpedo

bombers, and thus were unable to launch more planes. Then at 9:30 the dive bombers from the *Enterprise* and *Yorktown* appeared. They were flying at 19,000 feet, far above the Japanese fighters, which had gone down low to attack the torpedo bombers.

Some of the American bombers carried 500-pound bombs and some carried 1,000-pound bombs. The first carrier to be hit was the flagship *Akagi*. She was hit by three bombs. Soon she was aflame and Admiral Nagumo and the others on the bridge had to slide down a rope to escape the carrier. They were taken off by a destroyer and moved to the light cruiser *Nagara*.

The Japanese carriers *Kaga* and *Soryu* were also hit by bombs, one of which blew up the ship's bridge and everyone on it.

The dive bombers from *Yorktown* attacked the *Soryu* and put three 1,000-pound bombs into her.

The *Akagi* burned all afternoon and was finally sunk by a Japanese destroyer's torpedo. The *Kaga* also burned. The *Soryu* crew was able to put out the fires on that carrier, but in the early afternoon she was torpedoed by the American submarine *Nautilus*, and the fires broke out again. She sank at about 7:30 that night. So did the *Kaga*.

The Japanese still had one carrier intact, the *Hiryu*, and her planes took off around 11 A.M. and flew out to attack the *Yorktown*. They were led to the American carrier by two reconnaissance planes. They found the *Yorktown* just as she was preparing to take aboard her dive bombers. When the radar operator reported that 30 to 40 planes were coming in, the *Yorktown* speeded up to 30 knots and began to maneuver to escape attack. American fighters of the combat air patrol shot down half the Japanese dive bombers, but eight got through to drop their bombs. Three bombs hit the carrier. One dropped down the smokestack, and the explosion knocked out all but one of her boilers. Speed dropped to six knots. Another bomb knocked out the ship's communications system, so Admiral Fletcher moved to the cruiser *Astoria*. The damage control parties put out the fires and got the boilers working again, but a second strike from the *Hiryu* came in and put two torpedoes into the *Yorktown*. The carrier was abandoned.

That afternoon planes from the *Enterprise* attacked the *Hiryu* and she was hit by four bombs. She burned all that night and sank the next day.

So the Japanese attack on Midway had not brought success, but disaster. That night Admiral Yamamoto ordered the Midway occupation force to stand back, and he hurried to join the carrier force, even though there were no more carriers. He announced that he would still occupy Midway and would pursue the American ships and attack them with his surface vessels. Admiral Kondo, the commander of the surface forces, was told to prepare for a night engagement with the Americans. But Yamamoto, who believed that the Americans had four or five carriers, realized that he was likely to be the target of a dawn air attack, so he rescinded the orders.

The carrier *Yorktown* was abandoned after the torpedo attack, but she continued to float and the damage control parties said they could save her. The destroyer *Hammann* came alongside, and her crew was providing power for the work when the Japanese submarine *I-168* torpedoed them both, and they both sank.

While the battle was going on, the carrier *Saratoga* arrived at Pearl Harbor from San Diego. She refueled and moved out to meet the American task force and deliver her aircraft to the *Hornet* and the *Enterprise*. They were then to go north and engage the Japanese force that was attacking the Aleutians, but on June 11 Admiral Nimitz recalled the carriers, suspecting a Japanese trap up north.

So the Japanese had proceeded with the next part of their plan, to capture Midway and subtract it from the American perimeter and add it to their own. And they had failed. What remained was the last part of their plan, the occupation of the Aleutian Islands.

CHAPTER NINE

Alaskan Defenses

Back in the days between the two world wars, General Billy Mitchell, the air power advocate, had predicted that one day the Japanese would try to invade the United States and that they would do so by way of the Aleutian Islands and Alaska. But by 1937 very little had been done to prepare defenses for Alaska or the Aleutians. In 1937 Rear Admiral Ernest J. King, who was then commander of fleet aircraft, had secured a few thousand dollars in the navy budget for the building of a seaplane base at Sitka. After the Japanese scrapped the London Naval Agreement of 1934 and began furiously building naval vessels, a special commission, the Hepburn Board, reported on American defenses and stated that much was needed. Out of this report came a recommendation for expenditure in Alaska.

Later Congress appropriated $19 million for improvement of the Sitka base and to develop seaplane and submarine bases at Dutch Harbor and on Kodiak Island, southeast of the Alaskan Peninsula. In 1939 the only army tactical force in Alaska was a garrison of 400 soldiers which was two rifle companies, at Chilkoot Barracks near Skagway. That year the navy had the Sitka base and a direction finder station at Soapstone Point on Cross Sound and at Cape Hinchinbrook on William Sound. The navy also had a radio station at Dutch Harbor and a Coast Guard base. The construction of the new naval facilities did not begin until the European war started, in September 1939. In the summer of 1940 the contract was enlarged to include a naval air station and army defense facilities at Dutch Harbor.

The continued aggressive actions of the Japanese in

China, the occupation of Hainan Island, the takeover of bases and occupation of northern Indochina, all stimulated the American navy and army to new action regarding Alaska defense in 1940. The War Department in 1940 decided to build up the Alaska garrison, to establish a major army base near Anchorage, to develop a network of airfields in Alaska, and to provide troops to protect the naval bases at Sitka, Kodiak, and Dutch Harbor, but the actual buildup of bases was slow. Only when the Alaska Highway opened for traffic in late 1942 was the total dependence on air or sea travel around Alaska ended. In 1940 only two railroads were in regular operation, one of them the narrow gauge White Pass and Yukon Railroad, which ran from Skagway to White-horse in the Yukon Territory of Canada. The other railroad was the Alaska Railroad, which was owned by the government and operated by the Department of the Interior, extending 470 miles from Seward to Fairbanks, by way of Anchorage. Early in 1941 the army built a new airfield with a 5,000-foot runway on Otter Point on the northern end of the island of Umnak, not too far from Dutch Harbor. But it was so unstable that pilots said their planes would bounce 30 feet in the air when they tried to land, "like landing on an inner spring mattress." That field and a number of staging fields coming up from the Puget Sound area were operated by the Eleventh Air Force. They had little to work with. The army had only two aircraft radar sets in all of Alaska.

As of 1940 the army established the Alaskan Defense Command under Brigadier General Simon Bolivar Buckner. The navy created the Thirteenth Naval District with head-quarters at Seattle. The headquarters flagship was the gun-boat *Charleston*, and three small fishing vessels converted to patrol craft comprised the Alaskan navy. By May 1941 the American navy had, to defend Alaska, two old destroy-ers; one 240-foot Coast Guard cutter and two 165-foot cut-ters; some more converted fishing boats; and 10 Catalina flying boats, one at Dutch Harbor and one at Kodiak, and the others all in the south. Only the *Charleston* was equipped with sonar. This was the situation in Alaskan waters in May when Admiral Nimitz learned from the radio intercepts and the breaking of the Japanese naval codes that the Japanese were planning some sort of operation in the Central Pacific and that a venture into Alaskan waters would be a part of it. On May 17 Nimitz had formed the North Pacific Force, which consisted of the heavy cruisers *Indianapolis* and *Louisville*; the light cruisers *Honolulu, St. Louis*, and *Nashville*; and 10 destroyers. All this force was placed under the command of Rear Admiral Robert A. Theobald. It was called Task Force Eight, but in May it existed only on paper. The actual ships were strung out all over the Pacific. The army was alerted to the coming danger, and on May 27 Admiral Theobald reached Kodiak although his ships would not show up for another week. Theobald spent that week consulting with army and navy officers and putting together his defense organization. The main body would consist of the five cruisers and four destroyers that would patrol south of Kodiak. The "Alaskan navy," comprised of the patrol craft, would watch for the enemy and signal their approach. The air search group, which now consisted of 20 Catalina flying boats and one B-17, would fly daily searches from Cold Bay, Sand Point, and Dutch Harbor. The air striking group of 65 army fighter planes and 20 medium and heavy bombers would attack enemy ships from Kodiak, Cold Bay, and Umnak. Nine destroyers stationed at Makushin Bay, Unalaska, would strike at enemy forces, and six submarines were disposed around the area to watch for the enemy.

As of nearly the end of May, no one had very much information about the coming of the enemy, except that the Japanese intended to launch an air attack first of all, but where it would be was still a mystery, and what the Japanese plan involved was also a mystery. Where would they land, and what was their purpose? Were they setting up an advance base for invasion of the American or Canadian northwest? After the Pearl Harbor attack the authorities in Washington thought that anything might happen. And army and navy officers, including Admiral King, thought the Japanese might be planning an invasion of the West Coast. That idea was given credence by a number of sightings of Japanese submarines off the Oregon coast and in the Columbia River in May. For that reason, most of the air power of the Americans in the West was retained on the West

Coast, hundreds of army planes that could have been used in the Aleutians were kept on army air fields or were sent out to try to find and attack Japanese submarines. Meanwhile Admiral Theobald waited for his ships to arrive and also for the Japanese.

CHAPTER TEN

When the Japanese Came

The Japanese program for the invasion of the Aleutians was completely defensive in nature, although the Americans did not know that and suspected the worst. The Doolittle raid had sent shivers up and down the spines of Japan's leaders, for the one thing they feared as much as invasion of the home islands was bombing, which they knew would burn up their wood and paper cities. Prime Minister Tōjō had promised the Japanese people that they would never be bombed, and here, in the first year of the war, they already had been.

As much as the Americans, the Japanese were nervous about the intentions of their enemies. Admiral King insisted on the maintenance of the old battleship fleet, now largely salvaged and repaired, on the West Coast as protection against Japanese invasion. The Japanese high command suspected that the Americans were building an invasion force in the Pacific Northwest. Looking at the map, they could see that on a great circle course, Attu Island, the western bastion of the Aleutian chain, is only 650 miles from Paramushiro, the Japanese base in the Kuriles. So the fear became father to the thought.

What if the Americans were planning action? That was the reason for their dispatch of submarines to scout the northwest coast of America in the spring of 1942. The Japanese navy sent one of its long-range submarines, the *I-26*, to scout the Seattle area. The *I-26* launched the airplane it carried while off the Washington coast, and the pilot reported that he had seen no buildup of warships. The navy high command was very much relieved. To be sure that no such buildup occurred, the Japanese planned to use the Aleutians bases and Midway as bases for long-range aerial patrols. These islands would also delineate the new Japanese defense perimeter, which was also to be extended to Samoa, the Fiji Islands, and New Caledonia in the south.

The Japanese appreciation of the state of defenses of the Alaskan command was also highly inflated. They thought the Americans had large bases on all three of the islands they proposed to capture. They also believed that the navy was operating one or two carriers and several cruisers and destroyers in Alaskan waters. At the beginning of the war the army garrison for Alaska numbered 21,500 officers and men. In the next five months this figure was increased to 40,500. Most of these troops were engineers brought to Alaska to build the new Alaskan air bases. It was this activity that aroused Japanese interest. As for the physical defenses, before the war there were no combat aircraft at all in Alaska. It was January 1942 before the first two squadrons, one of fighters and one of medium bombers, were beginning to come up using a string of air bases built by the Canadians. A number of these planes crashed on their way north. By March only half the fighters and a quarter of the bombers were in Alaska and fit for combat. The number of crashes was so high that it impelled President Roosevelt to order the Alaska Highway built that spring. By the end of April Alaska had a squadron of fighter planes, a squadron of medium bombers, and one B-17. These were all stationed at Anchorage and Kodiak. Plans had been made to increase the radar installations in Alaska, but there were not enough sets available. Thus, on the day that the Japanese attacked the Aleutians only one radar was operating, and that at Cape Chiniak on Kodiak Island. But in May 1942 four radar-equipped heavy bombers arrived, which made the offshore patrols more efficient. That was the army's major means of detecting the approach of an enemy to the Aleutians.

Despite the spate of recent activity in the Alaska commands, in the spring of 1942 Dutch Harbor's army garrison consisted of fewer than 5,000 troops and the navy contingent was less than 750. The Japanese thought the American army had stationed an entire division at Dutch Harbor. Kiska, one of their targets, was occupied by 10 unarmed sailors in a weather reporting station and defended by about 250 marines. Attu, a second island to be invaded, was occupied by missionaries Mr. and Mrs. Charles Jones and a village of Aleutian natives. The Japanese suspected that the island also harbored a wireless station, an observatory, and a garrison of some size, but they did not know how large. Aerial observation, which they tried to conduct that winter and spring, had failed because of the almost continual bad weather. They sent submarines up to take a look in April and got closer to the truth, but by that time the Midway–Aleutians plan had been accepted by the naval high command and it was too late to change it if they wanted to do so. If they had changed the plan, it would have been to capture Dutch Harbor, which the Americans feared and expected. But already the Japanese were suffering from the shipping shortage that would plague them all during the war. They had so many commitments in the South Pacific and on the China coast that all available shipping was needed to launch the Midway operation, and there was virtually nothing left over for the Aleutians except the small force that had been committed.

The American army as well as the navy had access to the intercepted information about Japanese intentions in the spring of 1942. The intercepts in April showed that the Japanese were concentrating striking forces at their Truk naval bases and in home waters. The admiral in command of the Truk bases requested information from Tokyo and charts of the close-in waters along the Alaskan coast as far east as Kodiak Island. The army interpreted this as a definite threat to Alaska. They already expected some kind of Japanese raid in retaliation for the Doolittle raid. Watching and listening, army and navy by the last week in May had a good idea of what was going to happen about Midway and the Alaska area, and they also had an idea of the size of the Japanese force that was coming. On May 21 General Marshall and Admiral King agreed that command of the

Alaskan defenses would rest with Admiral Theobald and that General Buckner would be responsible to him. Only if the Japanese captured a base in the Dutch Harbor area and if a Japanese invasion of the mainland seemed imminent would the command change. In that case, the command would devolve to the army as principal defenders of the continental United States.

Admiral Theobald's arrival at Kodiak on May 27 was the signal for meetings to cement the command relationships. General Butler announced that he had begun to move army planes forward to the new Cold Bay and Umnak air bases. Stockpiles of bombs and fuel had already been delivered here. By June 1 a B-17, six medium bombers, and 17 fighters had reached Fort Glenn on Umnak Island, and six medium bombers and 16 fighters had arrived at Cold Bay. That day the navy was operating eight radar-equipped patrol bombers from Dutch Harbor, and reinforcements were being moved from the continental United States to Alaska to bring the strength of the air force up to 10 heavy bombers, 34 medium bombers, and 95 fighters. Total army strength in Alaska on June 1 was 45,000 officers and men, with about 13,000 of them in the Aleutians area.

On May 28 Admiral Theobald learned from Admiral Nimitz that the Japanese Aleutians invasion force included one task group destined to take Kiska and another that seemed to be bound for Attu Island. Admiral Theobald did not believe this report. He was afraid that the Japanese would land somewhere between Umnak and Cold Bay and try to seize Dutch Harbor. So he decided to deploy his main naval force about 400 miles south of Kodiak, thereby to defend the eastern Aleutians and Alaska. When he learned that the Japanese force included two carriers, he was very much concerned because he did not have the force to cope with it. The army planes, flown by pilots who were not trained in flying over water, would not be able to provide air cover for Theobald's ships; the Catalina flying boats were suitable only for patrol and air search. If Theobald sought a surface engagement, he would be faced with the difficulty of dealing with carrier-based aircraft, too. But Theobald realized that he was going to have to rely on the army and navy air units.

The Army fighters and the Catalinas would locate the enemy ships and the army bombers would bomb them. That was to be the first line of defense.

By May 28 the P-40 fighters and bombers at Cold Bay and the P-40s at Otter Point, Umnak, were operating. The fighters were making search flights and so were the Catalinas, going out as much as 400 miles. Admiral Theobald wanted more flying boats, but just then he could not secure more from the mainland.

On June 1 Admiral Theobald left Kodiak in his flagship, the cruiser *Nashville*, and met the other four cruisers and four destroyers of the main body about 400 miles south of Kodiak. He expected the landings to be made at Dutch Harbor. By the time he arrived there, the Japanese had already made their first air strike, and because Theobald had guessed wrong about the site of the invasion, choosing not to believe Admiral Nimitz's intelligence estimate, the main body was out on a limb and never did get into action in the Japanese invasion of the Aleutians.

CHAPTER ELEVEN

The Japanese Attack

The Japanese plan for invasion of the Aleutians was issued by the Imperial Navy on May 5, 1942. The Aleutians invasion force was organized at Ominato, the naval base on northern Honshu Island. The two amphibious forces that would make the landings were trained on Mutsukai Bay and the shore of Hokkaido Island. On May 25 the Japanese carrier force sailed from Ominato. Two days later the Kiska contingent moved out but stopped at Paramushiro in the Kuriles before heading east. The Adak–Attu force left on May 28 and moved slowly to keep parallel to the Kiska force.

From the outset the Japanese ships were shrouded in fog and heavy weather that persisted as they crossed the Pacific. Vice Admiral Hosogaya headed the entire operation. He sailed in the flagship *Nachi* with a supply unit that went to Paramushiro and then left on June 2 and moved to the Japanese standby area in the south of the western Aleutians. At Paramushiro the navy prepared planes, patrol boats, and flying boats to move into Kiska after the landings were made.

Rear Admiral Kakuji Kakuta's Second Mobile Force would lead the attack with the small carriers *Junyo* and *Ryujo*, and two heavy cruisers and three destroyers. The carrier planes would strike Dutch Harbor and the ships would bombard shipping, planes, and shore installations at Dutch Harbor and on Adak.

The carrier force would also provide air cover for the occupation forces. One force consisted of an army detachment of 1,200 troops with a naval escort, which would occupy Adak Island, destroy the American forces there, and then move on to Kiska and Attu. A second force was composed of special naval landing force troops, 550 combat troops, and 700 labor troops who would occupy Kiska.

The Japanese striking force was sighted by an American patrol bomber early on the afternoon of June 2. They were about 400 miles south of Kiska, but the PBY pilot made an error in his calculations, so the report was of no help. That day the Americans in Alaska and at Pearl Harbor picked up an unusual amount of radio activity, which alerted them to the fact that the Japanese were up to something.

Early on the morning of June 3, in the summer half light of the north, Admiral Kakuta's force reached its launching position, 165 miles south of Dutch Harbor. The planes were launched just before 3 A.M. The Japanese fliers had some difficulties. Some of them got lost. The whole *Junyo* contingent turned back halfway to the target. So at about 5:45 that morning, 17 bombers and fighters from *Ryujo* only attacked Fort Mears and the naval installations at Dutch Harbor. They found clear weather over Dutch Harbor and a ceiling of 10,000 feet. The radar operator of the seaplane tender *Gillis* detected the approach of the Japanese air attack force and warned the other ships in the area. They went to general quarters and got under way, but the attack came before they could get out to sea. The Japanese swooped down on the fuel tanks, the radio station, the army barracks at Fort Mears, and the Catalina flying boats moored in the harbor. The attacks killed 25 soldiers and sailors and destroyed some barracks. Two of the Japanese planes were shot down by American antiaircraft fire. One pilot sighted five destroyers of the American group located in Makushin Bay and radioed the information to Admiral Kakuta, who launched a second air strike at about 9 o'clock in the morning. But by this time the weather had closed in, and none of the Japanese planes found the destroyers. The Japanese cruisers launched four seaplanes that flew over Umnak for observation. They were set upon by two P-40 fighters at Otter Point. Two of the Japanese planes were shot down and the other two were damaged and had to be junked when they got back to the fleet. The carriers and their escorting surface ships moved to a point 130 miles south of Dutch Harbor to recover the aircraft. Around noon they began to retire on a southwestern course. They were not sighted by the search planes.

Admiral Theobald's ships were about 500 miles away from Admiral Kakuta that day. Admiral Theobald was furious because although he was receiving radio news of the attacks, he could issue no orders because of the rule about radio silence. His aircraft could not find the enemy.

On the night of June 4 Admiral Kakuta fueled his destroyers and then changed course for Adak Island, which was to be attacked next. But the morning of June 5 dawned so foggy that he had to cut the speed of the task unit to nine knots. His weathermen told him the weather in the west would be even worse, but that the weather over Dutch Harbor was good. The admiral then canceled orders for the Adak strike and sent his planes again to Dutch Harbor.

The heavy weather over the task force again prevented the American search planes from locating the Japanese ships. Nor did the picket boats see anything. At 4 P.M. on June 4 the two carriers launched another attack group of 11 dive bombers, six high-level bombers, and 15 fighters. After they had taken off, an American search plane located the carriers, and several army bombers were sent to attack but got no hits and only a few near-misses. One B-26 medium bomber and one B-17 were shot down.

The Japanese carrier planes found the target and good weather again. They destroyed four new fuel tanks and a wing of the Dutch Harbor hospital and damaged an aircraft hangar. The beached barracks ship *Northwestern* was bombed and damaged, and eight more Americans were killed.

When the carrier planes rendezvoused over Unalaska to return to their carriers, they saw below them the new landing field at Umnak. Eight P-40s came up and shot down three planes from the *Junyo*. But in combat and operational losses the Americans suffered that day, too. They lost two P-40s and three bombers, and the navy lost six of its 20 PBY patrol planes.

When Admiral Theobald learned about the second strike

on Dutch Harbor he could no longer contain his irritation. That evening of June 4 he left the main body and sailed in the *Nashville* for Kodiak Island.

That night, which marked the end of the attack phase of the battle of Midway, Admiral Kakuta had new orders from Admiral Yamamoto, who was trying to turn the defeat of the day into a victory by ordering a night surface attack on the victorious American carriers, which had destroyed the four fleet carriers in the Combined Fleet. With only one light carrier left to him, Yamamoto ordered Kakuta to come south to rendezvous with Admiral Nagumo's force, and Yamamoto announced that the invasion of the Aleutians was temporarily postponed. He began assembling the forces around him and also called for the Aleutian screening force of cruisers to come south. But by 7:30 that night Yamamoto had learned that there were three American carriers in the Midway force, not just one as he had been given to believe, and he realized that his chances of making a successful surface attack were extremely limited. So he reversed his orders and told Kakuta that the Aleutians invasion must proceed on schedule.

The Kiska and Adak occupation forces had already turned back according to orders and now had to turn around once more. It was the afternoon of June 5 before Admiral Kakuta reversed course and headed back for Alaskan waters, but the Kurita force was now a long way from Alaska and was ordered to stand by, about 600 miles southwest of Kiska. That put the carriers out of the Aleutians action.

Admiral Theobald arrived at Kodiak Island very upset. He immediately radioed Admiral Nimitz that he must have more air support or was in danger of losing the Aleutian Islands. Admiral Nimitz put the wheels in motion to get more air power to Alaska, but it would not come in time to affect the invasion of the Aleutians.

On June 5 Admiral Hosogaya decided that the invasion of Adak was not a very good idea, since the American airfield at Umnak was only 350 miles away. He canceled the order for the invasion and told Rear Admiral Omori, commander of the Adak–Attu occupation force, to proceed to Attu instead. Omori did so, and on June 7 landed 1,200 troops after sweeping the bay for mines and making a beach inspection. The Japanese landed at Holtz Bay and marched overland through snow to Chichagof. The main section of the detachment got lost on the trip and ended up in Massacre Bay. The Japanese charged into Chichagof and captured the missionaries Mr. and Mrs. Jones and 39 Aleutian villagers, 15 of them children. On the morning of June 8 the Japanese started to unload their transports and the unloading was finished by June 10.

The Kiska occupation force was supported by a seaplane carrier and a destroyer from Admiral Omori's ships and landed on June 7. The Japanese found and captured 10 members of the United States Weather Station there.

Now the Japanese realized that their whole Central Pacific plan had miscarried. Kiska was supposed to be the northern anchor of a new Japanese defense link, but without Midway it was useless. But Imperial General Headquarters decided to keep the occupation forces as they were, partly to forestall any American bombings and to keep an eye on American military buildup. Further, the success of occupying two more bits of American territory took some of the sting out of the defeat at Midway for the Imperial Navy. Before the end of June the Japanese were starting construction of airfields on both islands.

After the retirement of the Kakuta carrier force on June 4, the Americans in Alaska never did regain contact. In the next few days the American search planes were out constantly, looking but not finding. The Kakuta force was no longer within range. Early on June 5 an American search pilot made a completely false report about seeing two large carriers, two heavy cruisers, and three destroyers steaming from a point in the Bering Sea toward Dutch Harbor. Every available plane in the area was sent out to search and attack, but they could not find the illusory force. Admiral Theobald came to the conclusion that the report was true and that the Dutch Harbor strikes had been purely diversionary. Admiral Nimitz at Pearl Harbor ordered the carrier *Saratoga* to rendezvous with the carrier *Enterprise* and the *Hornet* and move north to counter this new threat. It was several days before

Nimitz realized that nothing was happening and rescinded the orders. In fact, something was happening about which he did not know. Admiral Yamamoto had ordered the Japanese carrier *Zuikaku*, the light carrier *Zuiho*, two battleships, and four cruisers to join Admiral Hosogaya's force, which included the carriers *Junyu* and *Ryujo*. Had Nimitz not pulled back, his carriers would have again been put at risk and perhaps surprised by a superior force. But since there was no encounter, this new Japanese striking force returned to home waters.

Admiral Theobald went ashore at Kodiak on June 8 to plan for the destruction of all these Japanese forces. It was not until June 10 that he learned it was all illusory. In disgust he decided he could not function from a flagship at sea and set up his headquarters at Kodiak.

The Japanese occupation of Kiska and Attu became known to the Americans almost by accident. The naval commander at Dutch Harbor, fearing the worst when reports from weather observers at Kiska and Attu suddenly ceased, sent the tender *Gillis* up to Atka Island, halfway between Dutch Harbor and Kiska. On the afternoon of June 10 a Catalina flying boat reported seeing four ships in Kiska Harbor and a tent colony on Attu Island. Thus the Americans learned about the landings that had taken place three days earlier.

When Admiral Nimitz learned of the occupation of the two islands, he ordered a submarine group to move into the Western Aleutians and the naval air command at Dutch Harbor to bomb the Japanese and force them out of Kiska. On June 11 the PBYs tried, using the tender *Gillis* at Nazan Bay on Atka Island. Army heavy bombers based at Cold Bay also participated. None of these attacks seemed to affect the Japanese on Kiska except to bring about a retaliatory air strike from several Japanese Kawanishi flying boats that had been moved in from Paramushiro. Warned of the Japanese coming, the navy moved the tender *Gillis* out of the area and to safety.

On June 18 the Americans scored their first success in

the Aleutians when army planes bombed and sank the Japanese transport *Nissan Maru* off Kiska. This was a foreshadow of the difficulties the Japanese were going to have in the following year.

CHAPTER TWELVE

Arctic War

In June 1942 the U.S. navy was making a determined effort to drive the Japanese from the Aleutians. The medium-sized American submarine *S-27* was one of the half dozen that had been assigned to operate in these North Pacific waters. Lieutenant H. L Jukes, her skipper, went out in mid-June to reconnoiter Amchitka Island for Admiral Theobald. At 11 o'clock on the night of June 19 he brought the *S-27* to the surface and lay five miles offshore to recharge her electric batteries. Fog closed in around the submarine, and she was swept onto a reef off Amchitka. The boat listed, the motor room flooded, and the submarine became filled with chlorine gas from the wet batteries. The crew sent out a radio distress call, but nobody picked up their position. The gas made it impossible to stay aboard the submarine, so the crew all went ashore in a rubber boat, carrying guns and supplies with them. They found an abandoned church and lived there for a week until rescued by Catalina flying boats from Dutch Harbor.

Soon Admiral Nimitz sent seven fleet submarines up to Alaska to assist in the patrols. On June 20 the *Growler* left Pearl Harbor and after a stop at Midway headed for her action station off Kiska. Lieutenant Commander Howard W. Gilmore spent three days watching Japanese aircraft but on July 5 the watch spotted three Japanese destroyers.

These destroyers were part of a task force including the carriers *Zuikaku*, *Ryujo*, *Junyo*, and *Zuiho* which were escorting a convoy to Kiska, built around the seaplane carrier *Chiyoda* and the transport *Argentina Maru*. They delivered 1,200 troops and six midget submarines to Kiska on July

3. The next day the submarine *Triton* found the destroyer *Nenohi* off Agattu and sank her. On July 5 the *Growler* met the other three destroyers, the *Arare, Kasumi,* and *Shiranuhi,* off the entrance to Kiska Harbor. The *Growler* approached and fired a torpedo at each of them, then launched a fourth torpedo at the *Arare.* The *Arare* replied with torpedoes of her own, which missed the submarine. Chased by patrol boats, she escaped on the surface into the mist. Then the explosions were heard. The two torpedoes had sunk the destroyer *Arare* and had damaged the other two destroyers. On July 7 the *Growler* was chased and depth charged by a persistent Japanese destroyer that damaged her propellers and sound gear. She finally escaped to the surface after darkness fell and soon was sent back to Pearl Harbor for repairs and reassignment.

At about the time that *Growler* was ready to go back to Pearl Harbor the *Triton* appeared in the Aleutians. She had arrived near Agattu Island (close to Attu) on July 4. Because of the weather the skipper, Lieutenant Commander C. C. Kirkpatrick, was not quite sure of his position and spent most of that day trying to get a navigational fix without any success.

That was the afternoon that the Japanese destroyer *Nenohi* came cruising by, steaming at nine knots, escorting a freighter. Kirkpatrick fired two torpedoes and dived. An explosion sent him to the periscope and he saw the *Nenohi* capsize, and then the fog lifted and Kirkpatrick was able to get his fix and find out that his dead reckoning had thrown him off by eight miles. The *Triton* stayed on station until July 12. Periscope problems sent her back to Dutch Harbor for repairs.

In obedience to Admiral Nimitz's demands, that spring of 1942 the American navy and army embarked on the bombing of Kiska, as well as they could. The primary problem was the weather, which offered constant difficulty. The first bombing offensive, which lasted from June 11 to June 13, involved the navy's PBYs and the army bombers from the field at Cold Bay. They managed to damage a destroyer and a few Japanese seaplanes in the harbor, but the losses were high. Three Catalina flying boats did not come back.

When the navy gave up because the PBY tender *Gillis* had to be moved out of Japanese air range, the army air force took over. In that first army mission a bombardier dropped a bomb from 15,000 feet, destroying the *Nissan Maru*, which was an enormous surprise to everyone. The Japanese were impressed enough that their seaplane tender *Kamikawa Maru* was sent out of the operational zone to Agattu, 90 miles to the west, out of the range of the American planes. So the bombing of Kiska was not a great success. Attu was not bombed because it was outside the range of the American bombers.

The bombing continued, although only on about half the missions flown in June and July 1942 were the pilots even able to locate the target. Those planes that did get through the thick weather did not accomplish much. Weather was the real enemy: in the summer and fall of 1942, 72 planes were lost by the Eleventh Air Force, only nine of them in combat. All the others were operational losses and most of them were due to weather. So after two months of fruitless bombing, the navy decided to try a new tactic. A naval force would try a shore bombardment of Kiska to force the Japanese out.

In mid-July, Admiral Theobald took his five cruisers and accompanying destroyers out of Kodiak Island toward Kiska. The *Triton* was still in the Aleutians area in August, and she went along to try to catch any ships that might be in the harbor.

On the night of July 21 the American force approached Kiska. It was very foggy but the ships managed to fuel from the tanker *Guadalupe*. Next day the fog still hung on and Admiral Theobald postponed the bombardment and started eastward. He returned on July 27 through more fog and again had to cancel the bombardment because of visibility problems. During retirement, two of the four destroyer minesweepers collided and a third was rammed by the destroyer *Monaghan*. With four crippled ships Admiral Theobald retired, and although Kiska Harbor was full of Japanese ships, none of them felt impelled to flee, so the *Triton* had no prey either.

CHAPTER THIRTEEN

Problems of Command

Planes of the Eleventh Air Force bombed Kiska as often as they could during the month of June. On June 12 six B-17s and one B-24 bombed the harbor and made extravagant reports of sinking a destroyer and damaging a cruiser. The next day four B-17s and and three B-24s bombed from 700 feet and claimed to hit three cruisers and a seaplane. Two B-17s were damaged but both made it back to their base. On June 15 a bombing mission was scheduled but was aborted because of the weather. The same thing happened on June 17. On June 18 the Eleventh Air Force claimed that a precision high-altitude attack on Kiska Harbor burned a transport. But two scout planes were shot down and one B-24 crashed at sea. On June 19 the B-24s taking off to bomb Kiska aborted because of fog. But one was lost when it was forced to make a water landing. For several days, then, the weather precluded any bombing. On June 26 the army planes dropped incendiaries on the Kiska Harbor installations.

On June 21 the War Department consolidated the supply program for the Eleventh Air Force bases, setting up a new command at Elmendorf to strengthen the system. Although the weather in the next week prevented almost all operations, a few were staged. One P-40 on patrol crashed in bad weather at Elmendorf on June 23. In spite of weather, however, several new squadrons appeared in the Alaskan area, as the air force continued to build up its forces.

In the middle of June 1942 the Joint Chiefs of Staff in Washington decided that a joint effort must be made to oust the Japanese from the Aleutians. Bombardment was not doing the job, and neither was naval action. The weather was just too bad too much of the time, and this was summertime. The first step toward some more positive action was taken on June 28 when submarines landed an advance reconnaissance party on Adak Island.

A major concern of the Joint Chiefs was the course the Japanese might be pursuing in this area. They thought it likely that the Aleutian occupation was a holding action to screen a Japanese northward movement into Siberia and the Kamchatka Peninsula. Admiral King and General Marshall warned that a Japanese attack on the USSR could also include attacks on Alaska, and particularly Nome and the airfields of the Seward Peninsula. General Marshall was disturbed enough that he ordered the rush movement of reinforcements to the Nome area, which was then guarded by a single infantry company. Twenty antiaircraft guns were brought up with their crews from Anchorage, and 140 plane-loads of men and equipment were flown in. By early July Nome's garrison was increased to 2,000 men. More reinforcements were brought to the north side of the Alaska Peninsula, and by mid-July the army had put intelligence detachments on St. Lawrence Island and in the Pribilofs to keep track of the Japanese.

On June 30 the War Department moved to strengthen the Eleventh Air Force, allocating two heavy bombardment squadrons, two medium bombardment squadrons, and one fighter group of four squadrons. The ground strength of the Alaska Defense Command was also strengthened, and by the end of August it numbered 71,509 officers and men. General John DeWitt, commander of the Western Defense Command, and General Buckner both expected the Japanese to act further, to make a new offensive to capture Dutch Harbor and more. They wanted to use army and marine troops to mount an expedition against Kiska as soon as possible.

Army and navy agreed on one matter—a new forward air base was needed. They could not agree on where it should be located. On July 2 a bombing and photography reconnaissance mission by seven B-24s and one B-17 to Attu came back to report that the island appeared to be suitable.

That was the navy choice for the base, but the air force indicated that it would take so long and require so much effort to build an airfield there that it should not be tried.

Almost every day in the first week of July the heavy bombers were attempting to fly bombing missions against Kiska and Attu and taking a look at others of the Aleutian chain to see if any Japanese had arrived there. They found no new bases, but the weather was so uncertain that they could not really tell. Most of their bombing missions were aborted or no observation could be made of the results because of low cloud cover. Both army and navy continued to lose aircraft, either to weather or to the enemy. The Japanese had brought many heavy antiaircraft guns to Kiska. On July 7 one more of the PBYs was shot down over Kiska. The Japanese did not confine themselves to attacks over Kiska, either. On July 11, just after a new squadron of B-24s arrived, Japanese seaplane fighters attacked the base as four B-24s were taking off. They shot up the planes on the runway, but no serious damage was done and in a few minutes they were gone. Japanese fighters continued to be very active. On July 20 a PBY reported being trailed by four Japanese fighters, and four P-38s took off to intercept, but they did not find the Japanese planes in the clouds.

It seemed always to be the same. On July 22 eight B-24s and two B-17s set out for Kiska again. Only eight of the planes made it to the target area; the others aborted. And the eight planes that bombed dropped only seven bombs. They could not see them land. To top it all, on the way home one B-24 got lost and was put down as missing. If the plane had gone down, there was scant chance that any of the crew would be rescued. Even in midsummer the waters of the Aleutians were icy. On the first bombardment mission against Kiska, one of Admiral Theobald's ships had one man go overboard. They stopped and recovered him, but he was dead of exposure after a few minutes.

So the Aleutians air war continued to be extremely dangerous in that summer of 1942.

Another week of bad weather was followed by continuation of the argument about the advance air base. As a result, more missions of survey were flown to Adaka and Tanaga islands.

The command situation was still not satisfactory. On July 20 General Butler moved his advance headquarters to Umnak Island.

On August 4, while escorting navy seaplane tenders to Nazan Bay, eight P-38s got into action, the first aerial combat of any of the new fighter interceptor planes in any theater. Two of them shot down two Kawanishi flying boats.

General Buckner planned for the occupation of Tanaga Island and construction of an airfield that could provide close support by land-based aviation. But that whole scheme collapsed when Admiral King perceived the threat to the South Pacific by the Japanese at Guadalcanal, and the Alaskan and Aleutian areas were relegated to a lower priority. No more forces would be made available, the army command was told. They would have to make do with what they had.

After Admiral Theobald's abortive attempt to bombard Kiska with a naval force in July 1942, he gave up the effort and turned the seagoing command over to Rear Admiral H. T. Smith. On August 3, 1942, Smith sailed from Kodiak with the same cruisers and destroyers, less the four crippled ships from the first attempt. On August 7 Admiral Smith decided the weather was good enough to make a close approach to the island, even though the weather where he was just then made navigation by dead reckoning necessary. That afternoon he plunged into the fog at 20 knots, and an hour and a half later emerged into clear weather. The cruisers put up spotting planes and moved ahead, but the water soon became shallow. Not knowing where they were because the fog had closed in again, the admiral backed off. That evening he made a second approach. The fog lifted, and the mountains of Kiska were ahead.

The ships moved in close enough to fire and began firing. The Japanese put up Zero fighters that chased the observation planes into cloud cover and kept chasing them, so that the spotting was not much use. The Japanese dropped a white smoke streamer that gave the shore gunners the range of the ships, and they began to fire too accurately for Admiral Smith's comfort. Just before 8:30 P.M. a submarine periscope was seen. The shore guns were firing too close for comfort and the cruisers had expended their ammunition allowance for the bombardment. Admiral Smith decided to haul out. One of their spotter planes got lost, and another plane was found to have 167 bullet holes in it.

The bombardment had seen some success. A barracks on the north side of the harbor was destroyed. Landing barges on the beach were destroyed. Three seaplanes were wrecked. A freighter was set on fire and later sunk by Catalinas, but two destroyers, three subchasers, and the six midget submarines were not touched.

So the bombardment was only minimally successful, and the army and navy commands could recognize that something larger must be done.

With the invasion of Guadalcanal the attention of Admiral Yamamoto was largely diverted to the South Pacific, and soon Admiral Hosogaya lost his aircraft carriers in the North Pacific. But the Japanese continued to be aggressive, putting up many seaplane fighters, the float version of the Zero, which performed like Zero fighters in the air. To help keep the pressure on Kiska, on August 24, 1942, General Buckner moved the 404th Heavy Bombardment Squadron up from Nome to the advance headquarters at Umnak.

What were the Japanese up to? On August 27 PBYs reported that the Japanese were beginning to transfer troops from their Attu garrison to Kiska. No one knew why.

Admiral Theobald decided that he wanted an airfield within fighter plane distance of Kiska so that bombers would be escorted on their trips. The army air force still wanted the base to be on Tanaga Island, located between Adak and Amchitka. Theobald did not like Tanaga because it had no anchorage and he argued for Adak, fifty miles farther east, which had an all-weather harbor. The quarrel developed and both sides appealed to the Joint Chiefs of Staff. They decided for Tanaga, assuming that it would take too long to build a strip at Adak. Theobald refused to give up. He declared that Tanaga offered a menace to navigation for the navy and apparently convinced Admiral King, who withdrew his support for the Tanaga plan. Faced with the choice of Adak or nothing, General DeWitt and General Buckner gave in, and ultimately General Marshall and the Joint Chiefs let him have his way. Adak it was. Preliminary reconnaissance landings on Adak toward the end of August revealed that there were no Japanese on the island. So on August 30 some 4,500 American troops began to come ashore at Adak. A tidal basin near the landing area was discovered to be suitable for an airfield. On August 30, in a violent storm, American troops occupied Kuluk Bay on Adak. The occupation was complete on September 1. Immediately the engineers started to build a runway. In less than two weeks the army engineers had a working airfield. The army made plans to increase the garrison to 10,000 men and to make it the strongest of the Alaskan bases.

The need for forward bases was clearly indicated on September 3 when the 21st Bombardment Group arrived to set up at Umnak. A bombing mission of six heavy bombers and five P-38 fighters set out that day to bomb Kiska, but five of the bombers and three of the fighters turned back because of bad weather. The other bomber and the two fighters went on. They bombed and strafed Kiska Harbor and claimed to have destroyed four seaplanes on the water. This was the longest attack flight yet carried out in World War II. The two P-38s that reached the target area had made a 1,260-mile round trip, and they landed back at Umnak with less than 40 gallons of fuel in their tanks.

After the Adak landing General DeWitt propoosed to send a force to St. Paul and St. George islands in the Pribilofs. Admiral Theobald indignantly protested this move so it was delayed, but ultimately DeWitt had his way and the army force landed on St. Paul September 19 and built an airstrip that was ready at the end of October.

The new base at Adak proved useful. On September 14 a force of 13 B-24 bombers, one B-17, and 28 fighters attacked Kiska in the first combined heavy mission. The fighters were P-39s and P-38s. The P-39s attacked three submarines in the water and the other planes attacked shore installations, especially the submarine base. The planes ran into heavy antiaircraft fire from the Japanese but the attack was very successful. Fighters strafing the Japanese installations hit three of the midget submarines as well as four motor Kawanishi flying boats. The B-24s also bombed some ships in the harbor and shore facilities. Two minesweepers and cargo vessels were declared to be destroyed, more seaplanes were destroyed, and fires were started in supply dumps. Two P-38 fighters collided in mid-air while chasing an enemy fighter.

On September 16 bombers operating over Kiska and Attu noted that the transfer of the Attu garrison to Kiska had been completed. What now?

The air force generals felt the need for more air bases in the area and began looking at Chichagof. On September 22 a reconnaissance flight returned to note that Chichagof was apparently deserted. At the same time a navy PBY landed at Amchitka with a scouting party that reported back to Admiral Theobald that Amchitka was not suitable for an airfield. The Japanese had been using it as an outpost, but only for a radio shack, which was destroyed by the bomber that day. This successful raid was followed by several weeks of very bad weather, and the attacks had to be suspended until September 25. At that time a combined American-Canadian air force group struck Kiska again. This first combined American-Canadian mission was a spectacular success for the Aleutians. The planes destroyed Japanese radar installations at Little Kiska and started fires in the main camp area where most of the Japanese troops were housed. P-39s strafed two submarines and several float planes in the water. The bombers returned to report that about 150 Japanese had been killed in the main camp.

Nearly every day for the next three weeks American and Canadian air force planes attacked Kiska. During September 116 tons of bombs were dropped on Kiska, which was twice as much as during the entire period from June to September. Several of the raids were especially successful, as one in which an ammunition dump was blown up and another in which six medium bombers sank a Japanese destroyer and damaged another. Air raids on Attu indicated that the Japanese had not abandoned that island as was earlier believed, and the bombers raided Chichagof Harbor again on September 28. Next day they were back and found a ship in the harbor which they bombed unsuccessfully. On September 30 they returned, noting that Attu camp had been enlarged, and they bombed that place as well as Kiska.

The Japanese were a little slow in discovering that the Americans had built an air base on Adak, but on October 2 they sent a bombing raid against the field. The bombers made a few holes but did no real damage.

In the first part of October the air force increased its activity over Kiska. On October 10 four missions of heavy bombers were sent to Kiska although the fourth one was diverted by weather. Every day in clement weather and sometimes not so clement the heavy bombers hit Kiska, destroying ships, planes, and ground facilities. But the Japanese kept on rebuilding and bringing in supplies.

But in November the weather turned very bad again and air operations were restricted until February.

That fall the army and the navy haggled about more bases. A proposal was made by the army to use Tanaga Island after all, but Admiral Theobald protested. The air force was upset because the pilots had noticed unusual Japanese activity around Tanaga, which might indicate the Japanese intention to take over the island and build an air base there. On September 6 a B-24 flying patrol had encountered a minelayer and tender near Tanaga, and had sunk the minelayer. The next day three B-24s that flew over Tanaga were attacked by three seaplane fighters. They shot down one of the Japanese fighters. So in spite of the navy objections to bases, the army continued to build up the air forces. On September 11 the 343rd Fighter Group was brought up to the Aleutians area to begin operations with three new squadrons. The runway at Adak was completed on September 12 and the field was ready for operations, so on September 13 the Twenty-first and 404th Bombardment Squadrons moved their B-24s up to Adak.

General Marshall suggested substituting Amchitka for Tanaga, and General Buckner arranged with Theobald to make a new survey of Amchitka. But the survey party did not proceed. Admiral Theobald said that its transport by PBY to Amchitka was too risky, in view of increased enemy activity in the area. What that activity meant, no one quite knew. The Japanese shuffling back and forth from Attu to Kiska had indicated that Attu might be abandoned, but it had been refurbished. On November 13 reconnaissance planes flying over Attu found a number of landing barges in Chichagof Harbor.

Bombers were sent the next day, but they could not bomb through the cloud cover with any idea of the results. On Novembver 16 delayed action bombs were dropped on Attu and Kiska but the results were not known. The Japanese were persistent, too. They increased the number of antiaircraft guns and seemed to move them around. On November 20 reconnaissance aircraft over Kiska drew heavy antiaircraft fire from Gertrude Cove. The Japanese also kept sending convoys to the Aleutians with supplies and men. On November 22 the bombers were alerted for a mission the next day against a five-ship convoy, but for two days the weather prevented any mission. On November 26 they did mount a mission, which found a number of ships in Holtz Bay. B-26s raided this shipping, escorted by P-38s. They claimed to have sunk one freighter. Two P-38s and one B-26 were damaged by antiaircraft fire.

The basic conflict between the air force command and the navy command continued. It had really become a conflict of personalities between Admiral Theobald and General Buckner, and there seemed to be no resolving it except by moving one or the other of them out of the picture.

Aside from the personality clash between Admiral Theobald, an outspoken and sometime cantankerous officer, and General Buckner, a major problem in getting anything done lay in the lack of communication between army and navy. Part of the reason had to be the split in the commands physically. The naval headquarters was located on Kodiak Island, and the army headquarters was located at Fort Richardson, near Anchorage, 300 miles away. A joint operations center set up by the army at Anchorage was useless and had to be replaced by a joint operations center at Kodiak. Until the center began to function in August 1942, the exchange of information between army and navy was virtually nil.

Army and navy had quarreled about command arrangements, and the navy complained that the army had been slow to give the navy support during the Dutch Harbor raid because of command difficulties. Not so, said General Buckner; the difficulty was in communications, not command. But the personality conflict between army and navy commanders had continued and dropped down to the lower levels. Not until orders from Washington forced the issue would the navy place its air operations under army air force command, which had been directed earlier from Washington. This sort of squabbling and quibbling had continued. Governor Ernest Gruening of Alaska and a special U. S. Senate committee urged that a unified command be set up in Alaska. The Joint Chiefs of Staff took up the matter and decided to do nothing. What was needed were some transfers of commanders. General Marshall talked about replacing General Buckner with a more senior officer. After months of this sort of conflict, in December Admiral Theobald was relieved of command and Rear Admiral Thomas C. Kinkaid took over. He and General DeWitt discussed the Amchitka matter and agreed immediately. They would build the airfield at Amchitka to keep the Japanese from doing so. That decision was reached on December 13 by the two when Kinkaid came to take over from Theobald as commander of the task force. Within a few days, Admiral King and Admiral Nimitz had agreed, and a reconnaissance party was on its way to Amchitka within the week. It looked as though a new era of cooperation between army and navy was about to begin in the strife-torn Aleutians.

So in the end it was the acidulous Admiral Theobald who was replaced, and almost immediately all the frictions died down.

CHAPTER FOURTEEN

The Japanese Problem

From the outset, the Japanese occupation of the Aleutian Islands had been a wasteful effort. The rugged and barren nature of the land created many problems, and the weather was as difficult for the Japanese as it was for the Americans. Kiska occupation was not pleasant duty.

The island is shaped somewhat like a caterpillar, as Samuel Eliot Morison described it in his *History of U. S. Naval Operations in World War II*. Kiska is four miles wide at its widest part, about three miles wide elsewhere, and 22 miles long, with a 4,000-foot-high volcano perched on the northeastern end. Halfway down the island, where the Japanese built their main camp, is Kiska Harbor, whose north and south heads form the protected shelter. Outside the harbor stands Little Kiska Island. All this area was ringed by antiaircraft guns. Because of the nature of the land, the Japanese had not built an airfield, and the basic air defense was from seaplanes, the float plane version of the Zero fighter. The four-engined Kawanishi flying boats, which the Americans called Mavis, became the basic bombing plane.

Most Japanese installations were built around the central area. In the south the most sheltered portion of the island was in Gertrude Cove, where the Japanese also had several installations, and a ring of antiaircraft batteries.

In August 1942 the Americans were surprised to see the Japanese moving troops from Attu to Kiska and wondered what was coming next. In fact the Japanese General Staff at that point had decided to abandon Attu and concentrate all their resources on Kiska. The entire Attu garrison was moved by transport and destroyer in three parts, between

August 27 and September 16. By this time the four aircraft carriers that had been assigned to Admiral Hosogaya had been taken away because the American invasion of Guadalcanal had directed the navy's primary attention elsewhere. But it was no problem, because the bad flying weather kept the Americans from really knowing what the Japanese were doing. The Japanese continued to supply the island then and maintained their "block" of American air operations from this area against the Japanese homeland, which had become the only purpose of the Aleutians command.

Occasionally a Japanese submarine came into these waters to scout the American forces and perhaps attack. The six midget submarines that had been delivered early in the occupation were put in the water, where they became an object of great interest to the American airmen. The bombers tried several times to sink them but without apparent success. But the midget submarines never got into operation in the Aleutians, because the weather and currents were too severe for them. Other boats did operate, some of the big fleet class I-boats and some of the smaller R-boats. On August 29 when the Americans were operating their PBYs out of Nazan Bay on Atka Island, the Japanese decided to eliminate that operation, so the submarine *RO-61* moved into Nazan Bay and torpedoed the American seaplane tender, the USS *Casco*, killing five men and wounding 20. The skipper beached the tender, and eventually she was recovered and taken to drydock in Kodiak. The submarine hung around these waters and the next day was bombed by a Catalina flying boat. The depth charge opened up seams in the submarine, and she began to trail oil. The American destroyer *Reid* came along, saw the oil trail, and followed it until she made contact by sonar with the *RO-61*. The *Reid* then began dropping depth charges. After two attacks the *RO-61* was so badly damaged that the submarine had to surface, and when it did the guns of the *Reid* opened up and finished the job of sinking the ship. Five Japanese survivors allowed themselves to be captured by the *Reid*, but all the other crew members preferred to drown in the spirit of the new Bushido.

As of about September 1 it became apparent to the Japanese and the Americans that the end of the ''good'' weather was approaching and that naval operations would mostly have to be postponed until spring—as would land operations. Every day that the weather permitted, the American bombers came over Kiska and inflicted some damage. Several destroyers were hit and had to be sent back to Japan under escort. Many flying boats and Zero-type float plane fighters were lost, but the replacements kept coming in from Japan.

Autumn and winter saw almost no active operations by Japanese or American naval forces. When the Guadalcanal campaign began, Admiral Theobald gave up the cruisers *Honolulu, Louisville*, and *St. Louis*. Six of the old four-stack World War I destroyers, which had been in the Aleutians, were sent back to the West Coast and converted to fast troop transports by the American navy, later to be sent to the South Pacific. So the Americans were not in a position to launch any naval action, even if the weather had permitted.

Fog and storms screened the Japanese from the Americans and vice versa. The Japanese did not learn about the existence of the new American airfield at Adak until October, and when they did, they could not do much about it. A few float planes made bombing raids on the airfield, but they were more of a nuisance than a threat. In clement weather the Japanese shipping in Kiska Harbor was always at risk from the growing number of American bombers, with their increasingly competent bombing crews. Several transports were badly damaged and some were sunk in the fall months. Some of the supply ships bound for Kiska were also sunk, as was the *Keizan Maru*, which encountered the American *S-31* off Paramushiro at the end of October and was promptly sent to the bottom.

With the transfer of the troops from Attu to Kiska, the Japanese garrison had proposed to settle down for the long winter night, but when Imperial General Headquarters learned about the Amerian occupation of Adak and the building of the airfield there, the generals and admirals got worried again about the possibility of another American invasion to match Guadalcanal. Perhaps, IGHQ began to believe, the Americans had revived the plan to invade Japan by way of the Kuriles. The sinking of the *Keizan Maru* by the *S-31* only sharpened their fears, and the decision was made to reoccupy Attu. The decision was confirmed by the sinking of *Cheribon Maru* in Holtz Bay on Attu on November 28 and the sinking of the *Kachosan Maru* in dock at Attu on November 27. On December 2 some 1,100 more troops arrived in Kiska and were transferred to Attu, where the garrison was restored.

By this time the American naval presence in the Aleutians was reduced to the light cruisers *Detroit* and *Raleigh*, four destroyers, and a handful of motor torpedo boats, plus the old Alaska navy's converted fishing boats. Obviously nothing was going to happen at sea for several months.

In the meantime the Japanese were worried about the future and the springtime. The Aleutians adventure had gone astray. The Guadalcanal adventure had gone astray. With the news that the Americans had built a new air base on Adak, the Japanese knew that they must strengthen their forces in the Aleutians and prepare to cut the American communications line to the Aleutians. Otherwise they would have to evacuate. And to evacuate the Aleutians, as the sinking of the *Keizan Maru* off Paramushiro showed so clearly, was to open the Kuriles to the possibility of American invasions and the establishment of American air bases to bomb Japan.

CHAPTER FIFTEEN

Enter Admiral Kinkaid

In the fall of 1942 the major American effort in Alaska and the Aleutian Islands was to prepare for an offensive to sweep the Japanese out of the Aleutians in the spring. On Adak Island army engineers and Seabees built hangars, warehouses, piers, drydocks, barracks, and other facilities and planned to handle 15,000 men. On Atka Island they built an emergency air strip. They started plans for another air strip on Tanaga. At Sand Bay on Great Sitkin Island, they built ammunition storage facilities and oil tanks.

The Japanese were hoping that winter to build at least two air bases, one on Amchitka Island and the other on Shemya Island. For the latter, they had expected to use the troops that were sent to the Aleutians in the fall of 1942, but the air raids of late November persuaded Admiral Hosogaya to land the troops on Kiska instead. As for the Amchitka base, the Americans beat them to it. After many discussions between army and navy, in December 1942 the Joint Chiefs of Staff approved an airfield for Amchitka, an island with a good harbor, 140 miles west of Adak, and only 80 miles east of Kiska.

Following his trip to Alaska in mid-December, Admiral Kinkaid took command of the naval forces on January 4. At the same time Admiral Smith was relieved as commander of the cruiser strike force in the Aleutians, and Rear Admiral Charles H. McMorris took over. He had been plans officer for Admiral Kimmel in the Pacific Fleet command just before the war, and then had commanded the cruiser *San Francisco*.

In November the air attacks on the Japanese-held islands

continued as often as the weather would permit, but starting in the middle of December the air force stepped up its activity in anticipation of landings on Amchitka. On December 30 a large group of B-25 bombers and P-38 fighters made a low-level attack on Kiska against two ships and three submarines found in the harbor. The Japanese sent up a number of Zero-type float fighters and shot down two of the P-38s, while four Japanese fighters were scored as probably shot down. One of the B-25s was shot down off Little Kiska. A PBY swooped down and picked up the survivors, but failed to return to base. Later that day B-24s, B-25s, and B-26s attacked Kiska Harbor again.

The B-24s were back the next day, but for the first few days of January the weather was too foul for flight operations. On January 5 the planes of the Eleventh Air Force sank the *Montreal Maru* off Kiska and the *Kotohiro Maru* off Attu when they were bringing in reinforcements for the Japanese. Again the weather closed in but on January 12 the fliers were in the air again, and this time they were covering the landing of an army garrison led by Brigadier General Lloyd E. Jones to occupy Amchitka. Four transports, escorted by destroyers, took the troops into Constantine Harbor. Admiral McMorris's cruiser force, now augmented by the *Indianapolis*, supported this operation. Three cruisers and four destroyers were involved. They did not encounter any Japanese opposition, but the destroyer *Worden*, while landing an advance force of scouts, ran aground on a sharp rock that punctured her engine room. She was dead in the water and drifting onto a lee shore. The destroyer *Dewey* tried to tow her clear, but the towing cable broke. The ship broached in the high seas on the shore, and the captain ordered the ship abandoned. The water was rough and the temperature was 36° Fahrenheit. Fourteen men of the crew died in the Arctic seas.

The Japanese soon became aware of the new American base on Amchitka, and it confirmed all their fears about the future. Early in February, Imperial General Headquarters, occupied with the withdrawal from Guadalcanal and new planning to restore their perimeter in the Solomons and New Guinea, had to take time to consider the Aleutians problem.

It was a "damned if you do and damned if you don't" sort of situation. Their loss of ships in the Guadalcanal campaign had been so serious that the army transport service was in tatters, nor did the navy have adequate transports. But Imperial General Headquarters was certain that they could not abandon the Aleutians. The generals and the admirals decided they must hold the western Aleutians and make preparations for an American attack against the Kuriles. Admiral Hosogaya was ordered to build airfields and prepare for action in the spring. He sent Pioneers to Kiska to build an airfield there. In mid-January two transports loaded with construction materials and supplies arrived in Kiska Harbor. The Eleventh Air Force then mounted an attack by B-24s, B-25s, B-26s, and P-38s on January 18 out of Adak. Bad weather closed in on both islands and the bombardment was canceled, but fierce weather caused the loss of six returning aircraft. On landing a B-24 crashed into two P-38s, and three other B-24s never made it back through the weather. The crew of one of the B-24s was rescued. It had crash-landed on Great Sitkin Island, and the men were picked up by a navy tender. As for the other B-24s, search missions were flown for a week, but no sign of them was found. On January 23 the weather was so foul that 13 aircraft were lost on that single day.

Despite bad weather at the end of the month both American and Japanese air forces were very active, the Japanese raiding the new base at Amchitka several times and the Americans concentrating on Kiska. The Japanese sent up several fighters to intercept the American bombing raids on Kiska and Attu, and the Japanese also sent fighters to strafe Amchitka installations and four-engine flying boats to bomb. But usually the bombing attempts were very badly carried out, as if the Japanese pilots did not have much taste for the missions.

In January and February the Japanese worked frantically on the airfield they were building southwest of Salmon Lagoon on Kiska. The Americans first became aware of it in a bombing raid when strafing P-40s went down low and caught sight of the strip. On February 9 a bombing mission was scheduled against the airstrip by heavy bombers and

B-25s escorted by P-38s. The bombers saw hits on the landing strip near the hangar. It was a race then to build air facilities for the change in the weather. On February 16, 1943, the American air strip at Amchitka was finished enough to take planes, and a P-40 having some trouble on a mission landed safely there. An afternoon patrol of P-40s and a transport plane also landed on Amchitka that day. Next day the metal matting was supposed to be laid on the strip to finish it, but the weather was so foul that the project was canceled for the day.

The army air force continued to pay close attention to the Japanese fighter strip on Kiska, bombing it at every opportunity, but sometimes they could take no action, as on February 22, when 16 bombers and eight fighters set out but had to abort the mission before reaching Kiska because of foul weather.

The Japanese were also building an air strip on Attu, but this had not come to American attention by mid-February. More important was the attention paid to Attu by the U.S. Navy. Admiral Kinkaid sent Admiral McMorris's cruiser force to sea to cover the approaches from Japan to Attu and Kiska. While at sea, Admiral McMorris had a report from the submarine *S-28* about new shipping having just arrived at Attu. On February 18 he made a run in to the Attu shore, arriving at about sunrise to find the best weather he had seen in weeks. The admiral was flying his flag in the light cruiser *Richmond*. Coming up to the island, they passed in column by Holtz Bay and Chichagof Harbor, searching inshore for ships, but all those transports had already departed for Japanese waters. That afternooon, so as to make something of the mission, Admiral McMorris decided to attack the shore installations. The spotter planes aloft reported seeing very little except a snow-covered plateau that rose up to the rugged mountains. All the gunpits and trenches seemed to be deserted. McMorris decided to bombard them anyhow and opened fire at five-mile range. They never did discover if they were hitting anything, although they fired for two hours before McMorris put an end to it and they retired to the north. They had not hit anything important; the Japanese had concealed and camouflaged their installations. One building had been destroyed and 23 men were killed.

After this bombardment, Admiral McMorris then split up his cruiser force and destroyers for patrol against Japanese shipping. The *Indianapolis*, with the destroyers *Coghlan* and *Gillespie*, was sent 120 miles southwest of Attu. That night an officer on the bridge of the cruiser and a lookout saw a ship's funnel glinting in the moonlight. It was the *Akagane Maru*, carrying a load of ammunition for Attu. The *Indianapolis* challenged the ship and when the reply came in Japanese, the cruiser opened fire on the ship, about three and a half miles away. The third salvo set the ship afire. The captain of the *Indianapolis* then ordered his destroyers to torpedo the vessel. But those were the days when Americans were having great trouble with the magnetic exploders on their torpedoes. The *Coghlan* fired a torpedo that struck the ship but did not explode and another that passed ten yards astern, and a third torpedo that exploded prematurely in a burst of spray. The *Gillespie* then took a turn. She fired torpedoes. One failed to explode, the second porpoised and missed. The *Coghlan* now came up and began trying to sink the vessel with gunfire. The *Coghlan* fired another torpedo that exploded prematurely. Finally at about 1:30 on the morning of February 19 they managed to sink the Japanese ship with gunfire. All the commotion had alerted two other Japanese cargo ships also heading for Attu, and when they saw what was happening they fled back toward Japan without unloading their cargoes.

Admiral McMorris's other section of ships had no such adventures, and in a few hours they were heading back to Kodiak.

That month, after reading the reports of the bombardment mission against Attu, Admiral Kinkaid concluded that an invasion of Attu would be much easier than an invasion of Kiska, and he so advised General DeWitt. Given the problems of the day, with Guadalcanal now safely in hand, but with a whole new operation beginning up the chain of the Solomons, to Munda and heading for Bougainville, Admiral Nimitz was not putting a very high priority on operations in the Aleutians. The North Pacific Force had as its objective the destruction of the Japanese force on Kiska but it did not have the shipping, the supplies, and the men available to carry it out. The Joint Chiefs of Staff told DeWitt and Kinkaid that there was no chance they would be given the men and materiel in the immediate future. Admiral Kinkaid and General DeWitt talked it over and concluded that Attu should be substituted for Kiska in the first operation because it would take a small force of men and not many ships. On March 18 Admiral Nimitz had the go-ahead for this operation from the Joint Chiefs of Staff, and the invasion of Attu was set for May 7, during what everyone hoped would be the height of the good weather.

CHAPTER SIXTEEN

Wearing Down the Enemy

On the last day of February 1942 an American reconnaissance mission flown over Kiska, Buldir, Semichis, Attu, and Agattu Island showed that the Japanese were still quiescent. To keep them so, six B-24s and six B-25s bombed the main camp area on Kiska between Kiska Harbor and Salmon Lagoon. The next day the P-40s were scheduled to work the area over with antipersonnel bombs and strafing, but the overcast was so heavy over the island that the fighter-bombers jettisoned their bombs and returned to base. They returned to make the raid on March 3.

That was the day that Admiral Kinkaid and General DeWitt agreed to postpone the invasion of Kiska and as soon as the weather changed to invade Attu instead. Since Attu had an airfield, courtesy of the Japanese, the capture of the island would put the American forces astride the Japanese line of communications between Kiska and the Kuriles, and Kiska could then be dealt with in the future when more ships and men would be available. Meanwhile after the capture of Attu, Kiska would be even more isolated than now, and the Japanese would find it almost impossible to supply the base.

Recent air reconnaissance photographs of Attu indicated to the American high command that only 500 Japanese troops were on the island. (That estimate was wrong; there were more than 2,500 Japanese on the island.) Such a small force as the Americans imagined to exist would not take many troops for invasion.

Japanese strength on Kiska had been estimated by Admiral Nimitz at 10,000 men so when they had been discussing Kiska, General DeWitt began planning for an invasion force built around a whole infantry division, with 25,000 men involved. He had already selected the officers he wanted to be in command: Major General Charles H. Corlett as commander and Brigadier General Eugene M. Landrum as assistant commander. Both officers had participated in joint amphibious exercises with the navy and both were familiar with conditions in the Aleutians. General DeWitt had suggested using the Thirty-fifth Division, but the War Department wanted to substitute the Seventh Division which was in a better state of readiness and was stationed at Fort Ord, California, which was the site of the army amphibious warfare program.

That spring a joint army-navy planning staff was established at San Diego under Rear Admiral Francis W. Rockwell, the commander of Amphibious Force, North Pacific. Major General Albert E. Brown, the commander of the Seventh Division, was made commander of the landing force. Those troops were just then training in the amphibious training course conducted by Major General Howland M. Smith of the Marine Corps, who had been brought in to manage the program for training all the amphibious operations that were scheduled for the Pacific in the near future.

The winter operations of the air force in the Aleutians had been very costly. (In January only a little more than 10 tons of bombs were dropped and the cost was 10 aircraft, all to operational difficulties.) In February and early March the weather had improved, but the real change had been the basing of P-38 and P-40 fighter bombers at Amchitka. They could take advantage of the short periods of good weather to mount and complete a mission from there when the opportunity arose. In February the Eleventh Air Force had managed to drop 150 tons of bombs.

And now in March the weather was improving, although

sometimes the change seemed imperceptible to the fliers engaged in combat operations.

After the decision was made on March 3 to table the Kiska invasion, the air force wanted to devote more attention to Attu, but the air buildup on Kiska was proving to be something of a threat, and so the tempo of operations there also had to be kept up.

For two days the weather prevented bombing, and on March 6 when a single B-24 flew over these same islands to look for signs of activity, particularly around the airfield sites of Kiska and Attu, nothing was moving. Still the American air force buildup continued, looking to the Arctic spring. The 343rd Fighter Group moved up to Adak. The first flight of medium bombers was brought in to Amchitka to begin operations. These two changes would enable the Eleventh Air Force to increase the tempo of its raids on Kiska and Attu. That day eight B-24s and four P-38s struck Chichagof Harbor and Holtz Bay on Attu. Later in the day a fighter sweep scoured Kiska, and six B-24s and 10 B-25s bombed North Head and the main camp area.

On March 9 the air force stepped up the action. Six B-24s, 10 B-25s, 12 P-38s, and four P-40s attacked Kiska in weather that changed moment by moment. The B-24s and the P-38s made their mission successfully against the main camp, North Head, and the Japanese submarine base. But by the time the B-25s and the P-40s arrived the weather was obscuring the island. Four of the B-25s managed to drop bombs but the other six and the P-40s returned to base without attacking.

That day Admiral Hosogaya set out from Paramushiro with a force of cruisers and destroyers and several transports to run the American blockade and deliver supplies to Kiska and Attu. Four days later the convoy reached the Aleutians, delivered the reinforcements and supplies, and departed within a few hours, unnoticed. Planes of the Eleventh Air Force had bombed Kiska on March 10 but had been grounded the next day because of weather, and heavy bombers had been turned back on March 13, although P-40s concentrating on the airfield had managed an attack. They saw 14 aircraft parked on the airfield and strafed. On their return, a flight of P-38s was sent to attack again, but only three of them managed to make Kiska in very heavy cloud cover. They strafed more aircraft that had been landed by the Japanese on the beach, and one of the pilots sighted a submarine that must have been part of Admiral Hosogaya's reinforcement convoy.

Planning for the Attu invasion early in March, Admiral Kinkaid and General Buckner decided that they would need only four attack transports (APAs) and two or three cargo ships (AKAs). On March 10 Admiral King had told Admiral Nimitz that the Joint Chiefs of Staff had approved the change of plan provided the Attu invasion could be carried out without committing more men and ships than were currently available. Even then the Joint Chiefs were not quite ready for a firm commitment. The army and navy could train for the Attu operation, but they still did not have a directive to do it. That had to await another major decision of the Joint Chiefs in consultation with Admiral King and Nimitz. What were they going to do this spring in the South Pacific?

Although Guadalcanal was in American hands, and on New Guinea Buna and Gona had been wrested from the Japanese by February 1943, logistics in the South Pacific and the Southwest Pacific were still tenuous for the Americans. General MacArthur was agitating for an amphibious force to carry out his operations against the Japanese on New Guinea. Admiral Halsey was eager to be moving up the Solomons chain. All this was under discussion at Pearl Harbor early in March when representatives of the South Pacific and Southwest Pacific commands flew to Hawaii to meet with the staff of the Pacific Fleet. Admiral Halsey had just occupied the Russells Islands, where instead of the thousands of Japanese they expected to find they encountered virtually none. The war in the South Pacific and Southwest Pacific was on hold, except for air and submarine operations, pending some decisions by the Pacific Fleet and the Joint Chiefs of Staff. All this was going to affect the course of operations in the Aleutians, too. As if to emphasize the need for some affirmative action regarding the North Pacific, on March 15 the augmented Japanese air force on

Kiska became more active. Three Japanese fighters attacked the weather plane that flew over the island in the morning. In retaliation the Eleventh Air Force staged a raid by B-24s and B-25s with fighters flying top cover. They bombed the main camp and the hangar area of the airfield. Their air cover fighters then came down to strafe. They did not encounter any Japanese fighters, but one of the P-38s was lost to antiaircraft gunfire. That raid finished, another strike of B-24s and P-38s then attacked the main camp and North Head. Up on top were four P-40s lying in wait for Japanese fighters but the Japanese did not come up. Later in the day B-25s escorted by eight P-38s made another strike on Kiska.

On March 16 the Japanese were more aggressive. Two attack missions of B-24s and B-25s were flown to Kiska that day from Adak, well-covered by 32 P-38s. The Japanese did not try to interdict this powerful raid, but later in the day three more missions were flown from Amchitka by the medium bombers, against North Head, radar sites, and the submarine base. Several Japanese seaplane fighters challenged these missions; four bombers were damaged and one B-25 did not return. The American fighters shot down one enemy float plane and the pilots claimed two more probables. The next day the Eleventh Air Force sent eight P-38s to Kiska looking for enemy fighters, but they did not make any contacts.

From Adak on March 18 six B-24s bombed the Kiska main camp area, six B-25s bombed North Head, and a dozen P-38s flew cover and then came down to strafe. More aircraft arrived at Amchitka airfield, and 12 P-38s were sent to attack the Kiska airfield.

On March 19 the Eleventh Bomber Command began operations at Adak, signaling a new buildup of bombing activity. On that day, too, Admiral Hosogaya set out on another resupply mission to the Aleutians from Paramushiro with the heavy cruisers *Nachi* and *Maya*; the light cruisers *Abukuma* and *Tama*; and four destroyers, the *Wakaba, Hatsushimo, Ikazuchi,* and *Inazuma.* They escorted the fast merchant cruisers *Asaka Maru* and *Sakita Maru,* which were also armed with deck guns. At sea they would make contact and bring in a slower transport that had sailed earlier, the freighter *Sanko Maru*, which had one destroyer as escort. Their destination was Attu Island.

CHAPTER SEVENTEEN

The Battle of the Komandorski Islands

During the last half of March the Eleventh Air Force increased the severity and frequency of its attacks on Kiska and Attu islands, usually making several air raids on them every clement day. The attacks were successful enough that the Japanese aircraft that were not destroyed were kept on the ground or hidden.

On March 26, 1943, Admiral Hosogaya's reinforcement and supply convoy reached the Aleutians area. The Americans knew they were coming, through the radio intercepts and breach of the Japanese naval code, and Admiral McMorris's task group was as ready as it could be.

Admiral McMorris had been cruising on a north-south line west of Attu for several days, waiting for the Japanese convoy to arrive. He was flying his flag in the light cruiser *Richmond*. The heavy cruiser *Indianapolis* had left the area and had been replaced by the *Salt Lake City*, which had been damaged in the battle of Cape Esperance in the Solomons, but had now been repaired and had received a new crew. The problem was that about half the crew was very green, just fresh from boot camp, and the ship had only been given time for one week of intensive target practice before moving into combat duty.

The cruisers were screened by the destroyers *Bailey*, *Coghlan*, *Dale*, and *Monaghan*.

At 7:30 on the morning of March 26, since the sun did not rise until 8:30 in the morning in these Arctic climes, it was cold, with the temperature just above the freezing point. This hour before sunrise Admiral McMorris's task group was 180 miles due west of Attu Island and 100 miles south of the Komandorski Islands. The ships were moving in a scouting line, six miles long, with the destroyer *Coghlan* in the front, followed by the *Richmond*, the destroyer *Bailey*, and the destroyer *Dale*. The *Salt Lake City* was next to last in the column and the *Monaghan* brought up the rear. The group was traveling at 15 knots and zigzagging as a precaution against submarines. As dawn began to break the lookouts could see fish coming to the surface of the water. The breeze was light, from the southeast, and the sky was relatively clear with a 2,500-foot overcast.

The ships' crews had just finished breakfast and were as usual going to general quarters. Then, almost at the same time, the *Coghlan* and the *Richmond* had radar contact with five blips. The five ships were then between seven and 12 miles to the north of the American group. The task group was alerted. Lookouts strained their eyes to see what was ahead. They saw what seemed to be transports, screened by destroyers and perhaps one light cruiser. It looked like a great opportunity for the American force against a vastly inferior enemy transport group. As the light grew brighter more ships continued to appear, but the Americans still anticipated a turkey shoot against what basically seemed to be a supply convoy.

Just after 8 A.M. the Americans suffered a rude surprise. A heavy cruiser appeared, larger than the *Salt Lake City*. Then another showed. In fact, both these Japanese cruisers outclassed the *Salt Lake City*, larger and longer and more powerful, making 35 knots to the *Salt Lake City*'s 32.5 knots. After the second heavy cruiser appeared, so did two more light cruisers, all coming up on the starboard bow of the American task group, while the transports and their destroyer screen steamed along on the port side. The Americans had run into Admiral Hosogaya's reinforcement force, which was at least twice as strong as their own. There would be no turkey shoot, but a real battle.

In the Japanese force, the heavy cruiser *Nachi* was in the lead, with the *Maya* following and the light cruiser *Tama* third in line, with the *Abukuma* and the destroyers *Wakaba* and *Hatsushimo* coming to do battle while the transports and their protective destroyers were on the other side.

At about the same time that the Americans made contact, the Japanese did, too. Admiral Hosogaya ordered his battle force to turn southeastward and engage the Americans while the two armed merchant cruisers continued on their way to meet the *Sanko Maru*.

At this point the *Salt Lake City* was at a definite disadvantage, well back in the line of American ships, three miles behind the *Richmond*.

What was Admiral McMorris to do now that the odds had changed so remarkably? If he engaged the Japanese force he was at a serious disadvantage against the larger and more powerful ships.

McMorris decided to hold the Japanese at long range and pursue and try to sink the Japanese transports. Meanwhile he called for help back to the Aleutians, where the Eleventh Air Force heavy bombers were waiting.

The McMorris report reached Adak Island where the American heavy bombers had just loaded up with antipersonnel bombs for the day's attacks on Kiska. General Butler estimated that it would take his planes an hour to unload the light bombs and replace them with armor-piercing bombs, and he started the process. The general also sent a message to McMorris suggesting that he fight a retiring action to the southeast, in order to move under the cover of the bombers. But the Japanese force was between the Americans and the Aleutians, and McMorris could not comply.

So almost immediately McMorris knew that he could not expect any immediate help from the air force in the Aleutians.

He decided to fight anyhow, mindful of Admiral King's impatience with commanders who did not take any opportunity to assault the enemy. And he turned over tactical command of the battle to Captain Bertram J. Rodgers, commander of the heavy cruiser *Salt Lake City*, which was much more likely to damage the enemy forces than his own light

Richmond. He would conform to the movements of the *Salt Lake City*, the admiral said.

The Japanese launched two spotting planes but the Americans did not put up any. Admiral McMorris decided to keep the *Richmond*'s plane for later use if necessary, and the *Salt Lake City*'s observation planes had just been degassed.

At 8:40 that morning the Japanese opened fire on the *Richmond* from a distance of 11 miles. The Japanese gunnery was good; on the second salvo they straddled the *Richmond*, but then shifted to fire on the *Salt Lake City*. The Japanese then concentrated their fire on the *Salt Lake City*. The *Salt Lake City* began to fire back, and on her third and fourth salvos she scored hits on the *Nachi* that started fires. One shell severed communications on the mainmast and the other exploded on the bridge, wounding 20 officers and men, and killing several others. But the Japanese damage control parties were at work immediately and the fires were quickly extinguished.

By the rapid change of course, and by moving between the Americans and the transports, Admiral Hosogaya had frustrated Admiral McMorris's plan to hit and run. Now it was just a question of running. The admiral changed course, turning 40 degrees to port and putting up speed to 25 knots. The Japanese responded immediately and increased their speed so that McMorris had to take the speed up to 28 knots, as the enemy pursued him on the port quarter.

The *Nachi* at this point suffered an electrical failure in her guns, but the *Maya* was firing steadily with her main battery. *Nachi* then launched eight torpedoes, but they were launched at extreme range and failed to make contact with the American ships.

The American flagship *Richmond* was still out of the range of her smaller guns and could not reach the Japanese cruisers, so Admiral McMorris conserved the ship's fire, but led the column zigzagging. To avoid the Japanese fire, Captain Rodgers was "chasing salvos" turning this way and that to confuse the Japanese gunners. The *Salt Lake City* concentrated her fire on the *Maya*.

The American destroyers moved ahead but did not fire, since they could not reach the Japanese anyhow. The Japanese light cruiser *Abukuma* and the Japanese destroyers were ordered to make a torpedo attack, but they delayed. Just after 9 A.M. the light cruiser *Tama* left the main formation. She steered between the American ships and the Japanese transports, and then she disappeared from the action.

The *Nachi* and the *Maya* made a sweep to the south to get between McMorris and the Aleutian bases. *Maya* then launched eight torpedoes. But at 9:10 she hit the *Salt Lake City*, destroying the starboard spotting plane. The shell killed two men and started fires. The plane was jettisoned over the side. The *Salt Lake City* was then hit below the waterline. A few minutes later the *Nachi* and the *Salt Lake City* slugged it out with their eight-inch guns. The Japanese cruiser slowed down and appeared to be smoking heavily. It had been hit by a five-inch shell from one of the American destroyers. The shell entered a gun port of the number one turret, exploded inside, and killed every member of the gun crew. Other five-inch shells burst above the main deck and killed a number of other Japanese sailors. The *Nachi*'s spotter plane was also apparently hit and damaged, although the Japanese said it continued to function all during the engagement.

All the Japanese ships at this time stopped firing. Admiral McMorris hoped that he had knocked out this cruiser, and he wanted to get a chance to sink the Japanese transports. He made a right turn to bring the American column around heading due north. But 10 minutes later, at 9:30, the *Nachi* damage control party had cleaned up inside the number one turret and it was firing again. The *Maya* and the four Japanese destroyers crossed the American wakes and began to pursue the American force. By 9:52 they were about five miles behind the American ships. The *Maya* and the *Nachi* were zigzagging to bring their guns into position to fire and also to beware of torpedoes that the American ships might launch at them in this stern chase. Admiral Hosogaya was concentrating on the *Salt Lake City*.

Captain Rodgers noticed that the Japanese light cruiser *Tama* had reappeared and come up to a point about 10 miles off his starboard quarter, and he asked permission to shift his fire to the *Tama* and soon did so. The *Salt Lake City* fired eight salvos at the *Tama*. The Japanese ship made a 360-degreee turn to evade the salvos.

At about this time Admiral McMorris heard from Admiral Kinkaid, who passed the information that the army bombers could be expected in about five hours. They had taken much longer than expected to switch over the bomb loads, and it was obvious that McMorris could not count on them at this stage of the action.

The *Salt Lake City* had been having trouble with her steering before the action, and now the problem was intensified just as the Japanese heavy cruisers began to find her range. The shock of her own gunfire carried away the hydraulic motor on the steering engine. The crew had suspected that some sort of trouble might develop and they had earlier rigged up a diesel boat engine that enabled the ship to make limited rudder maneuvers. After that the *Salt Lake City*'s movements became erratic. Still she kept firing from her after turrets against the Japanese.

The *Nachi* appeared to have recovered completely from the effects of those five-inch shells and closed the range to under 11 miles. She and the *Maya* were both throwing salvos at the *Salt Lake City*, and blue-dyed projectiles were falling within 50 yards of the *Salt Lake City*. They fired some 200 shells, but only one of them struck home, a high trajectory hit that penetrated the main deck and below the water line, then passed out of the ship.

At 10:15 Admiral McMorris had to give up his hopes of getting at the transports. *Salt Lake City* and the other ships were in too much jeopardy for that. The *Salt Lake City* was laboring, having trouble steering and taking water from the hit that had opened her up under water. Captain Rodgers asked for a smokescreen and Admiral McMorris ordered the destroyers to deliver it. *Bailey, Coghlan*, and *Salt Lake City* all began making smoke. Just before 10:30 Admiral McMorris changed the course of the American column to 240 degress to take advantage of that smoke. The Japanese were firing every time they got a glimpse of the *Salt Lake City* through the smoke. The Japanese light cruisers kept feeding information to the heavy cruisers about the American position, and the spotter plane kept at its work. The *Maya* fired four torpedoes, but none of the American ships was even aware of them.

At 11 A.M. Admiral McMorris's column was moving at 20 knots toward Kamchatka. The *Richmond* was leading, and the *Salt Lake City* was about a mile and a half astern of her. The four destroyers were grouped around the *Salt Lake City*'s port beam and port quarter, making smoke to conceal her from the enemy.

The battle had taken the ships to a point about 550 miles from Adak, and only 420 miles from the Japanese base at Paramushiro. Admiral McMorris was now worried because he knew it would be four hours before the American army air force bombers arrived on the scene, and it was possible that the Japanese might get an air strike much earlier than that to hit his ships. McMorris was also worried because the Japanese cruisers were making two knots more than the American ships.

McMorris then ordered a turn to the south inside the Japanese track. The *Maya* and *Nachi*, which could not see the American vessels because of the smoke, continued on course for several minutes, moving west, and when they turned the heavy cruisers and the light cruiser all fired torpedoes at the Americans. None of the torpedoes was effective.

At 11:03 the *Salt Lake City* was hit for the fourth time. This last shell caused flooding in the gyro room and the engine room. The damage control parties stuffed cloth into the cracks to stop the water. Soon the ship had a list of five degrees to port. She still kept firing and she still moved at top speed until the after fireroom went out of commission at 11:25. The speed of the ship fell to 20 knots, but then she recovered and speeded up again. Admiral McMorris ordered the destroyers to make a torpedo attack, but when he saw that the *Salt Lake City* seemed to be recovering, he canceled the order and the torpedo attack was not made.

But the *Salt Lake City*'s troubles were far from over. At 11:50 sea water in the fuel oil put out all the burners. Steam pressure dropped, power was lost, and the ship went dead in the water at 11:55. She was drifting. The ship at this point was 105 miles south of the Komandorski Islands and 190 miles west of Attu. The two Japanese heavy cruisers were only about 10 miles away on the port quarter and firing steadily at her. The light cruisers of the enemy were coming up on her starboard quarter. The Japanese destroyers were moving into torpedo range, and the *Hatsushimo* fired six torpedoes at the *Salt Lake City* at 11:54. The *Salt Lake City* was still firing with her after turrets, but she was nearly out of ammunition, and it seemed to be only a matter of time before the Japanese heavy cruisers sank her. When the *Salt Lake City* went dead in the water, Admiral McMorris ordered a torpedo attack from the destroyers to divert the enemy, and he began to move toward the *Salt Lake City* with the *Richmond*, to take off the crew of the stricken ship. The destroyer *Dale* came along to help. The *Salt Lake City* lay behind the smokescreen, invisible to the enemy. The destroyers *Bailey, Coghlan*, and *Monoghan* reversed course to deliver a torpedo attack against the two Japanese heavy cruisers.

They were moving into position five minutes later when the Japanese column suddenly turned and began to move west. Admiral Hosogaya was breaking off the fight.

The Japanese admiral was the victim of misinformation by his own forces. The *Nachi* spotter plane did not tell him that the *Salt Lake City* was dead in the water, and that pilot was the only one who could see that it was so. Admiral Hosogaya also expected the American heavy bombers to start arriving at any time. The Japanese had expended most of their ammunition and the whole force had been traveling at high speed, eating up fuel, and now the fuel supply was getting low. Already for Japan the problem of fuel was becoming worrisome in almost every engagement. And then the *Nachi* began to take five-inch shells from the destroyer *Bailey*. All three of the American destroyers, *Bailey, Coghlan*, and *Monoghan*, began to head toward the Japanese heavy cruisers, mindless of the many splashes from Japanese shells that were falling around them. They could not all miss, and one eight-inch shell exploded at *Bailey*'s starboard side. The captain ordered the crew to launch torpedoes, even though she was still six miles away, because he was afraid that the ship would be destroyed before he could attack. At 12:03 the *Bailey* got hit a second time by an eight-inch shell. This shell cut the electric power in the ship and the torpedoes were never launched.

The *Salt Lake City* was dead in the water for only four minutes thanks to the efforts of her damage control party. They cleared the salt water out of the fuel lines, connected other oil tanks, and relit the fires in the forward fireroom. The forward engines began to move. A few minutes later the ship was making 15 knots and gradually built up to 23 knots as power was restored throughout the ship. By this time the Japanese had turned away and the range was widening, so the *Salt Lake City*, which had been firing its after turrets, stopped firing.

By 12:15 the Japanese ships had disappeared over the horizon. The *Salt Lake City* had five feet of water in the after fireroom bilges but she was still capable of making 30 knots.

Seeing that the engagement was over, Admiral McMorris then set a course for Dutch Harbor, and as they ran homeward counted casualties and results. The *Salt Lake City* had lost only two men killed. The *Bailey* had lost five men. Twenty men in the task group had been injured.

When they reached port, the *Salt Lake City* and the *Bailey* headed south to Mare Island for repairs.

On the way home, Admiral McMorris was in touch with the air force and gave instructions on how the Japanese transports might be found. Several groups of bombers went out, but none ever connected. That afternoon two PBYs on routine patrol did sight the two Japanese transports, but the PBYs carried no bombs and their contact reports were inaccurate.

Only later did the admiral discover what had happened to the air force that day. The armor-piercing bombs they needed had been stored in various places and had frozen into the ice. Auxiliary gas tanks had to be installed in the B-25s. All this took four hours. Then a heavy snowfall hit Adak, and for two hours the weather grounded the aircraft. When the bombers finally did take off, they passed over the American task group but did not have enough fuel to pursue the Japanese. As for the Japanese transports and the freighter they were meeting, these ships gave up the attempt to land their supplies at Adak and headed back to Paramushiro.

Who had won the naval battle?

Radio Tokyo claimed a victory, but the Americans were used to that by now. The admirals in Japan did not think much of Admiral Hosogaya's conduct of the battle, and he was relieved of command within the month and sent into retirement for the balance of the war.

The reality of the battle was that the American force, outnumbered and outgunned, had prevented the Japanese from reinforcing Attu at a critical moment, and this was to have major impact on the whole campaign in the Aleutians.

CHAPTER EIGHTEEN

Attu

In the winter and spring of 1943 the men of the U.S. Seventh Division trained. They had been in Nevada, then moved to the amphibious center at California's Fort Ord. Both areas were as different from the Aleutians as they could be in climate and topography.

One of the most serious problems of the American commands was that they knew virtually nothing about Attu. Although it was an American possession, no one had bothered to map it properly, and the only available map was a Coast and Geodetic Survey chart, which showed only the land back to a thousand yards from the shore line.

From aerial photographs taken by the air force, a terrain model was constructed of the eastern part of the island, east of a line running from Temnac Cove to the ridge northwest of Holtz Bay. The model did not show the passes or the areas behind Henderson Ridge on the southeastern side of Massacre Valley or the interior west of Holtz Bay.

From Cape Wrangell on the western end of the island to Chirikof Point on the eastern end the island is about 40 miles long. At its widest point the distance is 20 miles. From the craggy snow-capped peaks that rise 2,000 to 3,000 feet above the sea to the beaches on the deep coastal indentations, small snow-fed streams flow into the sea. The valley floors are tundra, black muck covered with thick growths of lichens and moss. But whereas the tundra of Alaska proper is frozen most of the year, the Japan current runs close by the Aleutians, moderating the land temperature so that most of the time the Attu tundra is barely frozen, just enough for a person to cross on foot. That Japan current also keeps the island shrouded most of the time in thick fog, and the atmosphere seems to drip.

The eastern end of the island has four bays that break the land into lobes. The northern lobe lies between Holtz Bay and Sarana Bay. In the middle is Chirikof Point between Sarana and Massacre bays. The southern lobe lies between Massacre Bay and Temnac Cove. Steep valleys run back to the west into the mountains. Massacre Bay's valley is about a mile and a quarter wide at the beach front. It extends toward the mountains and a hogback rises in the middle, with steep sides. It rises to about 550 feet in altitude. The valley at Holtz Bay is also divided thus, but here the ridge extends to the ocean and the steepest part faces the water. About a mile and a half up the west side of the valley a low pass crosses this ridge into the eastern Holtz Bay Valley. Here it is possible to cross into the head of West Massacre Valley. A lower saddle separates the East Massacre Valley from the valley that leads to Sarana Bay.

Even after months of aerial photographic missions, very little was known about the harbors. The fog was so prevailing that much of the photography was useless.

By spring the Americans were aware that the Japanese had brought more troops into Attu. There were about 2,500 Japanese on the island by the time of the battle of the Komandorski Islands, which put an end to the Japanese attempts to reinforce the garrison. The combat troops included a battalion and a half of infantry, three antiaircraft batteries with 75-mm dual-purpose guns and smaller guns, and two platoons of a mountain gun battery with 75-mm pack howitzers. The service troops included a number of engineers who were building the airfield on the east arm of Holtz Bay. Colonel Yasuyo Yamazaki, commander of the island forces, maintained his headquarters at Chichagof Harbor, between Holtz Bay and Sarana Bay. Most of the island garrison was centered around Chichagof Harbor and Bay. A four-gun antiaircraft battery overlooked the west arm of Holtz Bay. Another battery was placed on the east arm of the bay. The third battery was part of the Chichagof Harbor defense. The mountain artillery men guarded the pass between Holtz Bay and Massacre Valley. Along the ridges that flank Massacre Valley and overlook Sarana Bay the defenders had located machine gun and mortar positions. So Holtz Bay and Chichagof Harbor were the most heavily defended positions.

The almost daily reconnaissance flights over the island showed some Japanese activity in the vicinity of Temnac Cove, Sarana Bay, and the Massacre Valley area, but it was almost impossible for the observers or the photographs to indicate the concealed Japanese positions. As always, the Japanese were masters at camouflage.

On April 1 Admiral Nimitz and General DeWitt issued orders for Operation Landgrab, which would be the invasion and occupation of Attu. By this time the intelligence estimates indicated that there were 1,800 Japanese on the island. So the plan for the landing force was increased by an additional battalion. The invasion force would consist of the Seventeenth Infantry Regimental Combat Team, a field artillery battalion, the Seventh Division's Reconnaissance Troop, a battalion of antiaircraft artillery, and a battalion of combat engineers. The Thirty-second Infantry was to be held at Adak as a floating reserve. It would be available for use at Attu on D-Day plus one. So the total strength of the American assault force would amount to 11,000 men.

As commander of the North Pacific Theater, Admiral Kinkaid would be in command of the entire Attu operation, which meant the shore-based air force, the naval escort, the cover, and the supply and service groups. Also the Fourth Infantry and one engineer regiment would occupy Shemya Island and build an airfield there. Rear Admiral F. W. Rockwell would be in direct command of the assault force. That included the naval air and fire support group, the transport group, a minesweeper group, and the landing force under Major General Albert E. Brown. When the troops were ashore, General Brown would assume command and the naval forces would stand offshore in support.

Since nobody knew precisely where they were going to land or what they were going to meet, several operational plans were prepared. Plan A called for the major landing at Massacre Bay with a smaller landing 600 yards west of the entrance to Holtz Bay. Plan B would have the major assault at Sarana Bay. Plan C called for landing the whole force at Massacre Bay. Plan D called for a landing of the main force at the west arm of Holtz Bay and another landing 600 yards west of the entrance. Plan E called for three landings, one on that same small beach, one in Massacre Bay, and one in Sarana Bay. The final decision would be delayed as long as possible, and more information would be sought when the force reached Cold Bay at the end of the Alaskan Peninsula, where the various units of the invasion fleet would assemble. Ultimately Plan E was adopted, with three landings, but Sarana Bay was eliminated and the main force would land at Massacre Bay. The main force was to march up the valley, seize the passes leading to Holtz and Sarana bays, and then move into the Holtz Bay area. There it would join a second force that would land on the north side of the island. Then the main force would move toward Chichagof Harbor while the northern force took the valley running from Holtz Bay. The planners assumed that in three days the battle would all be over.

Admiral Nimitz assigned three of the old Pearl Harbor battleships, then in San Francisco Bay, to this operation for gunfire support. The *Pennsylvania* had been renovated; she now had eight five-inch dual-purpose guns and the 40-mm quadruple-mount guns besides her 14-inch main battery. The *Idaho* and *Nevada* had not received so much attention but would add their big guns to the fighting force. An escort carrier, the *Nassau*, would provide carrier air support for the landings.

In the first two weeks of April the weather was too foul for much flying. Even the weather plane aborted several times. When they could the fighters and bombers raided Attu and Kiska, almost always encountering some opposition, particularly from antiaircraft guns, which shot down several fighters and bombers. They concentrated efforts around the airfields, and on April 17 the fighters strafed three airplanes parked on the Kiska field runway. On April 19 the fighters and bombers worked over four grounded ships in the Kiska submarine base area and set them afire. No more resupply convoys were coming in, but ships continued to arrive at both islands to resupply the garrisons, and the air force kept after them. As late as April 30 ships were still arriving at Kiska.

Late in April the Seventh Division went aboard transports in San Francisco and the naval force assembled at San Pedro. The whole operation was cloaked in secrecy, and a disinformation plan was put into effect to fool any enemy agents. An order was put out calling for a training exercise to cloak the movement of the troops. Medical officers lectured the men on tropical diseases, and the men wore their khakis. The winter clothing they would use in the operation was hidden. Naval officers made a point of studying charts of the North Atlantic and Cape Horn on the tip of South America.

On May 1 the ships assembled at Cold Bay below the snow-capped Alaskan mountains that surround the harbor. The place was deserted except for a group of wooden houses and Quonset huts, with no one around them. The airfield here was not visible from the harbor. In this lonely atmosphere the ships looked like a mighty armada: three battleships, three heavy cruisers, three light cruisers, one escort carrier, 19 destroyers, four attack transports, one chartered transport, and a number of support ships, tenders, tankers, minesweepers, and patrol boats. Here the army and navy officers conferred and adjusted their plans. Up north the air force concentrated its efforts on Kiska, not Attu. Admiral McMorris's cruiser force patrolled the western Aleutians, alert for another Japanese naval force. In spite of all the security the Japanese got the wind up, and somehow knew that the American attack was going to be made on Attu and not on Kiska. After the abortive effort with the two destroyers, Admiral Kawase, the new Japanese commander at Paramushiro, decided that he would delay his efforts to reinforce Attu until late May when the weather should be foggier than usual. The Japanese transports would by that time have radar installed.

Admiral McMorris's group had changed considerably since the battle of the Komandorski Islands. The damaged *Salt Lake City* had been replaced by the new light cruiser *Santa Fe*. The light cruiser *Detroit* joined up. Of the old destroyers only the *Coghlan* remained, but five new destroyers had been brought in.

The Japanese made a Guadalcanal-style effort to resupply Attu on April 10 with two destroyers, but they were sighted by a PBY that dropped several bombs. Fearing a full-scale air raid, the destroyers turned about and headed back for Japan.

On April 25 Admiral McMorris moved off the Attu shore and bombarded the island for half an hour with his force. That same day a Japanese lookout on the eastern Kuril island of Shimushu reported a large ship lying off the island. The Japanese sent ships and aircraft to find only a Russian minelayer setting mines in Soviet waters.

The weather, as usual, played tricks with the Attu invasion force. It was scheduled to sail from Cold Harbor on May 3, but the seas were so rough that day that the effort was delayed for 24 hours. The ships lay and tossed in the harbor, and waited.

CHAPTER NINETEEN

The Landings on Attu

On May 4 the Eleventh Air Force Thirty-sixth Bombardment Squadron began operations from Amchitka, increasing the attention that was now being paid to Attu Island. B-24s, B-25s, P-38s, and P-40s hit targets on Attu that day, concentrating on the antiaircraft guns at Holtz Bay and Chichagof Harbor and wrecking one float plane in the bay. That day the American assault force left Cold Bay in weather so rough that the battleships had to elevate their forward guns so the breaking waves would not rip off the muzzle covers. The flotilla steamed along the south side of the Aleutians, entered the Bering Sea by Amutka Pass, and steered widely out north of Kiska so as not to tip off the Japanese to the run-in point, which was 115 miles northeast of Attu.

The weather continued to be very rough, and scouting planes reported high surf around Attu, which was expected to continue through May 7, so Admiral Rockwell postponed the landing until May 9. Meanwhile the Japanese sent the *Kimikawa Maru* to Attu with some more aircraft, and the freighter and its accompanying destroyer delivered their planes and left. The American battleship force had gone off toward the Kuriles, hoping to find a Japanese naval force at sea, but there was nothing and they missed the two ships that had delivered the supplies.

On May 8 the weather continued so foul that the waves were sweeping over the 40-mm quadruple mounts on the battleships. Admiral Rockwell postponed D-Day again, this time until May 11. The fog was dense, which was good because it concealed the invasion fleet from prying eyes, but it was so dense that the ships ran the danger of collision.

They refueled on May 9. The battleships returned from their journey and the flotilla made ready to move to Attu. In the fog the ships moved very slowly, most of them trusting to their radar. The destroyer *MacDonough* got between the destroyer minelayer *Sicard* and the ship ahead of her, and was rammed by the minelayer. Both ships then headed for port, lost to the invasion fleet.

The American landings were scheduled to begin at 10:40 on May 11. That morning several air missions were scheduled for Attu. A B-24 was sent for liaison between the air forces and the ground forces. Other B-24s were to drop supplies to the ground forces. Still others were to make an attack mission on Attu in support of the landings. But the attack mission could not find the target and had to resort to bombing by instrument. The weather above Attu was so bad that the next two missions changed course and bombed Kiska instead. Later two B-24s did manage to bomb Chichagof Harbor in the fog, and one other B-24 dropped leaflets on the Japanese.

So the Japanese knew they were coming. Admiral Koga, the commander of the Japanese Combined Fleet, who had succeeded Admiral Yamamoto after the latter was shot down over Bougainville in April, had warned the Japanese garrison on Attu that the invasion was coming. So Colonel Yamazaki had two days' warning. Besides, the leaflets dropped that morning by the air force bombers had been picked up.

"Absurd leaflets," the Japanese said, "urging that we surrender."

Early on the morning of May 11 the American submarines *Narwhal* and *Nautilus* each sent about 100 scouts ashore in rubber boats on the northern side of the island to bring back information that would let Admiral Rockwell decide precisely where to land this segment of the troops. They landed on what they called Beach Scarlet. The destroyer transport *Kane* put about 400 troops ashore several hours later. These soldiers moved up the mountain valley searching for the pass to Holtz Bay. They reached the pass in midafternoon but found it was impassable. They dug in for the night right there. No information was sent back to the ships about Beach Scarlet.

On board the transport *J. Franklin Bell*, which carried the troops for the northern landing, Colonel Frank L. Culin fretted when he did not get any word. He took two landing craft to go ashore and do some scouting, each landing craft towing plastic dories. Aboard he had the Alaska Scout Detachment, which included some Aleutian Indians. The weather was so bad that they could only see ahead about one ship's length. Protected by a destroyer, the landing craft made their way through the fog, and the Aleuts got into the dories and then landed on Beach Red, just outside Holtz Bay. They looked for the enemy, but found no Japanese. They sent back word and six more boats came up filled with men, and landed the troops. So Red became the site of the northern landing, and by nightfall 1,500 troops had been put ashore here.

On the south side, the southern group of the expeditionary force was embarked in three transports, protected by nine destroyers and the battleship *Nevada*. This force was off Massacre Bay early on the morning of May 11. The ships put down their landing craft and embarked the troops. Fog closed in on the flotilla, and Admiral Rockwell ordered the landing delayed until the weather improved. The troops sat in the landing craft and waited. It was a warm day for the Aleutians, temperature at just about 50° Fahrenheit, and the sea was calm. After noon Admiral Rockwell decided that the landing would begin at 3:30 in the afternoon no matter what the weather was.

The first wave went in toward the beach, following the minelayer *Pruitt*. Two more waves went after. The fog began to lift, and by 8 P.M. 2,000 Americans were ashore at Massacre Bay. Their command posts were quickly established and their beachheads extended inland for a mile. There they expected to run into the Japanese.

But where was the enemy? The planes of the escort carrier *Nassau*, which had made several early morning air strikes on the island before the fog closed down operations, had seen no Japanese. A bombardment of Chichagof Harbor that morning had not aroused any response from the Japanese.

The enemy, in fact, had moved into the valley connecting Massacre Bay to Holtz Bay. With only 2,600 troops to defend the island, Colonel Yamazaki felt he had to concentrate his forces. The Koga warning, the leaflets, and the monitoring of American ship transmissions in the clear on invasion morning had given the Japanese plenty of warning. Yamazaki had burned all the secret documents at his headquarters and moved with the troops to his prepared defense position, ready not only to fight, but to fight to the death of every man.

At Paramushiro, Admiral Kawase also knew that the Americans were coming to invade Attu. He acted. The admiral sent three transport submarines to Kiska, rather than sending them to Attu. He ordered land-based bombers to attack the American transports, and he left Paramushiro in the heavy cruiser *Maya* with the escort of the destroyer *Usugumo*. He intended to join the *Kimikawa Maru* convoy. When he sailed he made arrangements to be joined by another heavy cruiser, two light cruisers, and two more destroyers. They were to join him as soon as they pulled into Paramushiro. Admiral Koga had assigned the heavy cruisers *Myoko* and *Haguro* to the Kuriles command, and they were on their way. The navy had also increased the land-based air force there and brought more submarines to operate out of the Kuriles. Admiral Koga also sailed for home waters to supervise the Aleutians fight, leaving Truk on May 16 in the battleship *Musashi*, accompanied by the battleships *Kongo* and *Haruna* and the carrier *Hiyo*. The cruisers *Tone* and *Chikuma* sailed a few days later from Truk. The carriers *Zuikaku*, *Shokaku*, and *Zuiho*; the heavy cruisers *Suzuya*, *Kumano*, and *Mogami*; and the light cruisers *Agano* and *Oyodo* were already in Japan. Admiral Koga intended to use these forces to challenge the Americans.

CHAPTER TWENTY

On Attu

It seemed that if anything could go wrong with the Attu invasion, it would. The Eleventh Air Force had made elaborate plans to support the invasion and to prepare the way for it. The air force had concentrated two dozen of its finest fighter bombers on Amchitka for preinvasion bombings of the island. In the first week the army planes dropped 95 tons of bombs on Attu. But the bad weather that postponed the landings had also stopped the attack missions and most of the support missions planned for D-Day.

By 9:30 on the night of D-Day, 3,500 Americans were ashore on Attu, 400 on Beach Scarlet, 1,100 on Beach Red, and 2,000 at Massacre Bay. The Northern Landing Force made contact with the enemy that evening at about 6 P.M. when a patrol moving along the beach at the foot of the escarpment encountered four Japanese soldiers a mile southwest of Goltsov Point. Two of the Japanese were killed but the other two escaped. Shortly afterward the patrol came under the fire of one of the dual-purpose guns at the head of Holtz Bay, and the advance was stopped. The Seventeenth Infantry First Battalion main element of the Northern Landing Force on the tableland above the escarpment had continued without being bothered. Its objective was Hill X, an 800-foot prominence two miles south of Beach Red. This camelback dominated the Japanese positions at the head of Holtz Bay. By 10:30 it was so dark that it seemed dangerous to move farther, so the troops dug in without quite knowing where they were. The fog came down and made it even darker. They hoped they were on Hill X.

The troops who had landed on Beach Scarlet, the Pro-

138

visional Battalion, had spent most of the day climbing up the sides of a steep stream. By midafternoon the advance unit had reached an elevation of 2,500 feet and seemed to be at the summit of the pass. This was the end of the map. To go on would be to get lost. Captain William H. Willoughby, commander of the Provisional Battalion, decided that they would bivouac for the night right there.

The Southern Landing Force ran into the enemy just after 6 P.M. and came under fire. The Second Battalion combat team of the Seventeenth Infantry was moving up the right side of the hogback there and along the floor of the valley. It had advanced 2,500 yards to the east when it was stopped by rifle and machine gun fire from the high ridge, Gilbert Ridge, that formed the east rim of Massaacre Valley. The battalion was pinned down for 45 minutes, but then began working forward under scattered rifle fire. As the men moved the fire became steadier and was joined in by mortars and light artillery fire. The battalion was stopped again. Any direction in which the men tried to move immediately drew fire. At 9 P.M. the battalion dug in for the night. They were along the east slope of the hogback, about 3,000 yards from the beach where they had landed five hours earlier. On their left, the Third Battalion had made about the same progress, having caught up when the Second Battalion was stopped by the Japanese. The Second Battalion was on the right side of the hogback and the Third Battalion was in the west arm of the valley. The enemy was in front of them, firing from the heights above the passes to Holtz Bay and Sarana Bay and from the ridges on the sides of the valley. The Third Battalion called for fire from the 105-mm guns that had been landed on the beachhead. The guns sent concentrated fire against the high ground, and the Third Battalion tried to resume its advance. But the moment the artillery fire ended and the battalion began to move, the Japanese began firing again. The Third Battalion then stopped and dug in. They were a little bit ahead of the the Second Battalion, which was on the other side of the valley. Two small detachments had been sent out onto the flanks to secure the ridges, Gilbert Ridge on the right and Henderson Ridge on the left. One of these detachments was a platoon of the Seventh Reconnaissance Troop. It landed on Alexai Point, four miles east of Massacre Bay beach, and halfway out the peninsula toward Chirikof Point. Its mission was to establish an outpost line across the peninsula from the point to Sarana Bay. It was to reconnoiter to the west and the east, in the direction of Chirikof Point. It was also to make contact with a platoon of the Seventeenth Infantry in the pass between Sarana Bay and Massacre Bay. That Seventh Reconnaissance Troop platoon had lost contact with the main landing force after landing on Alexai Point and did not make contact with the other platoon that night.

That second platoon, from Company F of the Seventeenth Infantry, had moved east along the shore of Massacre Bay and up the steep pass leading over Gilbert Ridge to Sarana Beach. It was reinforced with a light machine gun section and a 60-mm mortar squad. Its mission was to seize the pass and Gilbert Ridge, to establish a defensive position at the Sarana end of the pass, to control Sarana Beach and Lake Nicholas, and to clear the ridge of enemy troops. Its further mission was to assist the Second Battalion in the capture of the pass at the head of Massacre Valley. That platoon spent the night of D-Day climbing to reach the Sarana Beach side of the mountains.

A platoon of Company I of the Seventeenth Infantry had landed at Massacre Beach and had been sent to secure the valley side of the ridge. The going was difficult along the lower slopes, and fog and darkness halted the platoon. It had reached a point about 700 yards short of that position where the Third Battalion of the Seventeenth Infantry had dug in.

Farther out on the left flank, behind Henderson Ridge, Company F of the Thirty-second Infantry ran into a blind alley after reaching its first objective, Temnac Cove. It was delayed because it had landed farther to the east than it should have landed. But Company F reached Temnac Cove by nightfall. There an outpost was discovered and destroyed before the Japanese were aware that the approaching men were Americans. Company F then reported that its first mission, of clearing the Temnac Cove site, was accomplished.

General Brown spent much of the day aboard the transport *Zeitlin* off Massacre Bay waiting for the fog to lift and permit the landings to take place. When Lieutenant Colonel Albert E. Hartl, commander of the First Battalion, asked to get the rest of his troops onto Beach Red that morning, and Admiral Rockwell announced that the landings would take place fog or no fog, the general became very impatient to get off the ship and onto the beach. He went ashore toward the end of D-Day, well-satisfied with what seemed to be the results. The tactical situation was confused because of darkness and fog, but it did not indicate that any great difficulties had been encountered. The Southern Landing Force appeared to be close to its immediate objectives, the passes leading from the head of Massacre Valley to Holtz Bay and Sarana Bay. The Third Battalion of the Seventeenth Infantry reported that night that it was only about 600 yards from the Holtz Bay pass. The Second Battalion was believed to be within 1,000 yards of the pass leading to Sarana Bay. It seemed that the First Battalion had really reached its objective, Hill X. The Thirty-second Infantry's Second Battalion had not been committed, except for Company F. The other two battalions of the Thirty-second Infantry were due to arrive from Adak within 24 hours. If reinforcements were needed, the understanding was that General Buckner was willing to release the Fourth Infantry, which was being held at the moment to occupy Shemya Island as soon as Attu was secured so that the building of the airfield could begin.

So as night settled down over Attu on D-Day, General Brown had reason to believe that everything was right on schedule and that the island would be under control in a very few hours.

CHAPTER TWENTY-ONE

The Fight for Attu

On the morning of May 12 the Eleventh Air Force ran into foul weather over Kiska so it concentrated its efforts on Attu where the visibility was much better. Seven attack missions were flown by B-24s, B-25s, and P-38s that day. B-24s also dropped supplies to the troops on the beaches.

That morning General Brown was in for some surprises. Within the first two hours it became apparent that this was not going to be a walkover, but that the Japanese were prepared to give the Americans a long, hard fight for Attu. In Massacre Valley, the Second Battalion of the Seventeenth Infantry had misjudged, and was 500 yards farther from its objective than anyone thought. The Third Battalion had mistaken a blind valley for the Holtz Bay Pass, and it was more than 2,000 yards south of its first objective. Neither Gilbert Ridge nor Henderson Ridge had been cleared of the enemy, and so both these battalions came under fire from the flanks as well as from the front. The Second Battalion had been ordered to consolidate and hold its position to block the Sarana-Massacre pass. It was necessary to move forward over rough terrain under heavy fire. Colonel Edward P. Earle, the Seventeenth Regimental commander, was killed by machine gun fire while up with the forward element. Colonel Wayne L. Zimmerman was immediately appointed to take command, a move that cost General Brown his chief of staff. At the end of D-Day plus one the battalion was in position to block the pass, but the Japanese were still in their positions. The platoon from the Seventh Reconnaissance Troop, which had landed on Alexai Point, was still out of contact with the main landing force.

On the morning of D-Day plus one the platoon from Company F of the Seventeenth Infantry, which had been climbing all night, was on the Sarana side of the mountains, and there it was discovered by the Japanese, who began to make counterattacks in patrol strength against the Americans. The men struggled westward along Gilbert Ridge.

To the left of the hogback, the Third Battalion managed to move forward to the rising ground at the mouth of the Holtz Bay–Massacre pass. But there it was pinned down by the Japanese. Frontal attacks against the mouth of the pass failed that day, even though the Third Battalion now had the support of the Second Battalion of the Thirty-second Infantry. The First Battalion of the Seventeenth Infantry Regiment had reported taking their objective, Hill X, on D-Day but on the morning of D-Day plus one they found that the eminence on which they were dug in was the wrong one, and they were still 900 yards short of Hill X. Worse, the Japanese had occupied that hill during the night. The battalion fought hard all day long and won Hill X by evening, but the Japanese still occupied the reverse slope and the shoulders of the hill.

On D-Day plus one Company F, which had reached Temnac Cove, moved northward toward Holtz Bay to clear the enemy force from the flank of the main landing force advancing up Massacre Valley. But it made no progress, and finally that day found itself in a cul de sac. General Brown ordered the company to pull out and retrace its steps to Massacre Beach.

On D-Day plus two Company F did pull out and, fighting the Japanese in a rearguard action, moved back to the beach. On D-Day plus two the Third Battalion of the Seventeenth Infantry was still fighting at the mouth of the Holtz Bay–Massacre pass, assisted by the Second Battalion of the Thirty-second Regiment. The First Battalion was still trying to pry the Japanese off the reverse slope of Hill X. The Provisional Battalion was bottled up in the same position it had held for two days, a mile from the mouth of the canyon.

On D-Day plus two the other two battalions of the Thirty-second Infantry (First and Third) arrived at Attu and were thrown into the battle. General Brown said he needed more troops, and his staff officers agreed with him. Immediately they wanted the 501st Antiaircraft Battalion and the miscellaneous units of the Seventh Division, plus the Fourth Infantry Regiment, which General Buckner was still holding for the Shemya occupation.

On D-Day plus three General Brown assessed his situation and was not pleased with it.

"Reconnaissance and experience of four days fighting indicates Japanese tactics comprise fighting with machine guns and snipers concealed in rain washes or in holes or trenches dug in each side and at varying heights of hill along narrow passes leading through mountain masses," he said. These positions were difficult to find and almost impossible to destroy with artillery. They produced too many casualties. Also the Japanese had more machine guns than their numerical strength would indicate. Besides this, small groups of Japanese infantry were dug in high up on the sides of the passes, and on all commanding terrain features. The Japanese were making expert use of the cover of the land. Since the mountains were snow-covered it was very difficult to try to approach the positions on the sides of the passes from above.

The general anticipated that progress through the passes would be very slow and costly in terms of casualties, and that he needed many more troops to do the job.

On May 15 General Brown went aboard the *Pennsylvania* for a conference with Admiral Rockwell. He stated his case. At first Admiral Rockwell was not convinced that more troops were really necessary, but General Brown said he just could not guarantee any dates of victory without them. Rockwell, who had expected a quick victory as much as the general, was growing anxious about his naval force, stuck off the island for so long. He finally agreed reluctantly to forward General Brown's recommendations to Admiral Kinkaid with his endorsement in support. But General Brown did not really think he had Rockwell's support and wrote a message for General DeWitt, who was at that moment on Adak Island. Brown said he had made many attempts to get more troops without success and asked General DeWitt's intercession.

On May 15 Admiral Kinkaid joined Admiral Rockwell in concern over the situation of the naval vessels. On the night of D-Day a PBY had warned the *Pennsylvania* that a torpedo wake was headed her way. The battleship took evasive action and the torpedo passed by harmlessly. But the same thing happened again on May 15, and Admiral Rockwell was growing increasingly nervous. That day the destroyers *Edwards* and *Farragut* teamed up to hunt the submarine, along with a PBY, and they thought they had sunk her. But they had not. She got away even after she was brought to the surface by depth charges and then shelled. She submerged again, and the destroyer men thought she had gone to Davy Jones's locker. But they were wrong.

For four days the battleships, cruisers, and destroyers had been directing their fire at the beach. By May 15 almost all the ships had exhausted their bombardment ammunition. The closest place to get more was the ammunition ship *Shasta* at Adak. The Eleventh Air Force and the escort carrier *Nassau* flew as many missions as they could, but there were troubles. One B-24 carrying supplies for the ground forces ran into a mountain in the fog 10 miles west of the drop zone. Three fighter bombers were catapulted from the *Nassau*, but the planes ran into williwaws as they flew up the Japanese-held valleys, and three of the planes were lost.

Admiral Kinkaid was becoming very restless. The troops had only advanced about 4,000 yards. Who knew if the Japanese were not even now steaming toward the island with a large naval force? They had certainly been given plenty of time to assemble it. Admiral Kinkaid was very much disturbed by General Brown's repeated requests for more troops and more time. An officer of the *Pennsylvania* ashore on business heard the general predict that it was going to take six months to capture Attu the way things were going. Admiral Kinkaid had that word on May 15, but there was also some encouraging news. Colonel Cullin's Thirty-second Infantry troops came down off the mountain to report that the Japanese had left stores and weapons behind and had retreated from his area. Through a mountain pass from the west came the 400 troops who had landed at Beach Scarlet. They had been lost for five days and were suffering from frozen feet. But there was more bad news, too. That day four torpedoes were fired at the transport *J. Franklin Bell,* but all of them missed.

On May 16 the *Nassau* planes bombed and strafed the troops of the Thirty-second Infantry, not knowing who they were. The troops had no ground panels or any other way to indicate the front line. That day Admiral Rockwell withdrew three unloaded transports and stationed his fighting ships to the north of Attu to decrease the chances of attack on them. That evening Major General Eugene Landrum arrived at Attu in the destroyer *Dewey,* boarded the *Pennsylvania,* and reported to Admiral Rockwell that he had been ordered to relieve General Brown as commander of the ground forces. The battle had reached a crucial stage.

CHAPTER TWENTY-TWO

The Fall of Attu

On May 17, 1942, the Eleventh Air Force tried to carry out two ground support missions against Japanese positions on Attu but the weather had closed in over the island and prevented them from bombing.

On May 14 the naval units had stepped up their bombardment of the Holtz Bay area, and this constant attack persuaded the Japanese to withdraw from that area. Colonel Cullin's battalion and the Provisional Battalion moved into the west arm of Holtz Bay. After fighting almost foot by foot they took the high ridge that separated the two arms of the bay. The ridge fell on the night of May 16. This put the Northern Force of two battalions behind the Japanese who were defending Massacre Valley Pass. So on the morning of May 17 the Japanese moved out and withdrew toward Chichagof Harbor.

That day Colonel Cullin's battalion of the Thirty-second Infantry made contact with the Southern Force. Also early the next morning, May 18, the Northern and Southern Forces joined when a patrol from the Seventeenth Infantry's Third Battalion met the Seventh Reconnaissance Company on the western slope of the Holtz Bay–Massacre pass. Holtz Bay was cleared of Japanese, who had completed the retreat to Chichagof Harbor to make their last stand.

So was the relief of General Brown necessary? It does not seem to have been, for the tide of war had changed on the day, and almost at the late afternoon hour, that he was relieved by General Landrum. General Brown said later that the relief was totally unnecessary, and that it was done at Adak with unjustified assumptions about conditions on Attu.

147

He also said that those assumptions should have been checked before the irrevocable step was taken. Admiral Kinkaid's action resulted from his concern for the seeming lack of progress of the battle that kept his naval force at risk. It was true that Admiral Kinkaid had conferred with General DeWitt and General Buckner about the Attu forces being bogged down, and they had concurred in the relief. But it is quite possible that General Brown's ill-timed observation, obviously the result of frustration, that it might take six months to capture the island had been a deciding factor. The naval officer who overheard it and took the word directly to Admiral Rockwell must have been as worried as were all the other senior officers of the *Pennsylvania* after their experiences with the Japanese torpedoes and their concern about the possible coming of a Japanese naval fighting force.

On May 18 the battle went slowly. The Eleventh Air Force planes scheduled to make a ground support strike on the island were weathered out. Admiral Kinkaid had ordered the movement of the ships out of harm's way, and so only the destroyer *Phelps* and the gunboat *Charleston* remained to support the troops, and the seaplane tender *Casco* to service the Catalina flying boats.

Admiral Rockwell's force maneuvered north of the island. The Japanese had tried to make an air attack on the naval force on May 13 but the planes had been driven back by the weather. Thereafter every day for a week the Japanese shore-based air forces were ready to attack, but the 20 torpedo bombers had not been cleared for attack because of the continued heavy fog. The *Kimikawa Maru* could not launch her float planes, either. Admiral Kawase was at sea, but since the Japanese radio on Attu reported that American battleships and heavy cruisers were operating very close to the island, Admiral Kawase waited for reinforcements, and, waiting, he did not come within 400 miles of Attu, not wishing to risk his heavy cruisers against battleships.

On May 19 the Eleventh Air Force flew a number of missions to Sarana Valley, bombing the remaining Japanese there.

That day Imperial General Headquarters ordered Admiral

Koga to take his forces and seek battle against the Americans. The admiral was en route to Tokyo from Truk, and he could have brought a mighty force to Attu—several battleships, four carriers, at least three heavy cruisers, and half a dozen light cruisers. But by the time Koga arrived in Tokyo Bay on the night of May 21, the high command had a change of heart. It was occasioned by the reports from Radio Attu, which had given an exaggerated figure for the American naval vessels that had been operating off Attu. Imperial General Headquarters reversed its order and told Admiral Koga to stand by and await developments.

On May 22 the Japanese land-based torpedo bombers finally got clearance and headed for Attu. Nineteen twin-engined Betty bombers set out from Paramushiro. They were spotted by radar, but radio interference prevented the ships off Attu from getting warning, and they arrived at 3:48. The *Phelps* and the *Charleston* began to get up speed and maneuvered skillfully while sending up a barrage of anti-aircraft fire. One torpedo was exploded in mid-air by an antiaircraft burst, one Betty bomber was shot down, and another was crippled and later crashed at sea. The other 17 pilots returned to Paramushiro to report that they had sunk a cruiser and a destroyer and set a third ship afire. In fact all their torpedoes had been successfully evaded by the two ships, and they were only slightly damaged by strafing.

On May 23 the skies above Attu were clear part of the day, and the Eleventh Air Force flew a number of ground support missions to the Chichagof Harbor area where the Japanese troops were now concentrated. The planes involved were three B-24s and 18 P-38s, and in all they made three trips. On the last trip they were warned by a PBY that a flight of 16 bombers had been sighted west of Attu. Five of the P-38s peeled off, and as the bombers came in over Attu they attacked them and shot down five bombers, losing two P-38s. The other 11 bombers then jettisoned their bombs and returned to Paramushiro.

On the ground, Colonel Yamazaki's troops had taken position on a fishhook-shaped ridge commanding Chichagof Harbor and overlooking Sarana Bay. Colonel Zimmerman reorganized his Seventeenth Regimental Combat Team for the attack.

On May 24 the weather was too bad for the Eleventh Air Force planes to make much impact, although one flight of two B-25s missed a callback order from base and came in to bomb anyhow, with uncertain results. Later missions that day by B-24s and P-38s were all scrubbed.

On May 25 the Eleventh Air Force had better luck. A dozen B-25s and 15 B-24s made ground support missions successfully. Twenty P-38s flew air cover that day over the island, looking for Japanese air attacks, but none came. May 26 was almost the same.

On May 27 most planes were grounded, but one B-25 was over the American lines, dropping aerial photographs taken the day before that showed the disposition of the Japanese troops. With the help of those photos Colonel Zimmerman's men managed to capture the barb of the hook of the ridge.

On May 28 a PBY flew over the Japanese positions on Attu and dropped more leaflets, again urging Colonel Yamazaki's men to surrender. Again the leaflets were greeted with scorn, but they may have triggered the colonel's next action. That night the colonel led his men from the ridge to the plateau where the American forces were concentrated. At the first light of dawn, at about 3:30 in the morning, the Japanese made a banzai attack. A thousand Japanese charged through a gap in the American line. Some were armed with rifles and bayonets. Some had samurai swords. Some had grenades, some brandished pistols, and some had only bayonets roped to sticks. With these weapons and automatic weapons they charged forward, screaming:

"Japanese drink blood like wine."

"American you die."

"Tenno heika, banzai."

The Japanese overran two command posts. They killed Lieutenant Colonel James Fish at one of them. They charged into the medical station, stabbing wounded men and the chaplain.

Finally they were stopped by a detachment of engineers wielding rifles and automatic weapons. When surrounded, the Japanese began to kill themselves with grenades or tried to rush forward to explode a grenade against an American. Driven back, they regrouped and launched another attack, and another. The battle continued all day long. By nightfall the Japanese were exhausted and the Americans nearly so. Next morning the Japanese remnants launched another banzai charge, and all who were not killed then killed themselves.

Not knowing what had happened on Attu, on May 29 Imperial General Headquarters ordered an evacuation similar to that of Guadalcanal and prepared the naval forces to make it. Admiral Kawase's Fifth Fleet was ordered to make a feint north of the island to draw the American warships in pursuit, while a number of destroyers entered Chichagof Harbor to take the Japanese off. But when Radio Attu went silent and the next day the Japanese heard American radio broadcasts announcing the end of the battle, Imperial Headquarters canceled the orders.

That was the end of organized Japanese resistance on Attu. The Japanese lost 2,351 men killed and gave up 28 prisoners. They killed some 600 Americans and wounded 1,200. The actual figures were not known, but *Time* correspondent Robert Sherrod counted the American graves, which came to 565. Besides those men buried, some had drowned in the landings and some had died on the way to hospitals or in the hospitals.

CHAPTER TWENTY-THREE

The Battle for Kiska

During those fierce last hours of the Japanese on Attu, many examples of heroism by American soldiers emerged. For conspicuous gallantry and action beyond the call of duty, Private Joe P. Martinez of Company K of the Thirty-second Infantry was awarded the Medal of Honor posthumously. Colonel Zimmerman received the Distinguished Service Cross for his leadership of the Seventeenth Infantry Regimental Combat Team. Twelve distinguished unit citations were also awarded the army forces involved in the action. More important for the war effort were the lessons learned about amphibious warfare. The Attu operation was, after all, only the third operation. Guadalcanal and the North Africa landings had gone before.

The loading and unloading of the transports was done clumsily. The naval bombardments were delivered from too long a range. The Seventh Division had been trained for desert warfare and the hurry-up training program initiated at San Diego had not been enough to make them proficient in Arctic climes. But they had learned, and in the Marshalls operation to come the Seventh Division would function like clockwork in the capture of Kwajalein Island.

The fall of Attu was greeted with enormous relief by the Americans, particularly on the West Coast, who still had visions of a Japanese assault on the American mainland. But the Japanese on Kiska remained—many, many more of them than there had been on Attu—and the American high command turned its attention to Kiska and the problem of knocking the Japanese out of the Aleutians altogether.

To the Japanese, the Attu garrison's sacrifice was an

example of the new Bushido that the leaders said would win the war for Japan. *Gyokusai*, "shattered diamond," they called it. This sort of suicidal defense was extolled by the Japanese government and in the press. It all went back to the *Senjinkun*, the code of conduct to guide the Imperial Japanese Army, written by General Tōjō in 1941 when he was war minister of the Konoye government. Ultimately the suicidal assault would be refined into the *tokko tai* special attack corps and the kamikaze flights of the Japanese air forces. The Japanese ambassador to the Soviet Union reported to the Foreign Ministry that Premier Stalin had been deeply impressed by the Japanese sacrifice. He obviously wanted it to serve as a model for the Russians in their battle with Nazi Germany, so he ordered the story of Attu's suicidal defense to be included in Russian textbooks. In terms of comparison, the Japanese defense of Attu was deadly to the Americans. Only in the battle for Iwo Jima were American casualties higher by percentage of American troops employed. For every 100 enemy troops on Attu, 71 Americans were killed or wounded.

But what were they to do about Kiska? As the battle for Attu ended, the Japanese high command realized that the battle of the Aleutians was becoming too expensive to maintain. They now expected the Americans to increase their attacks on Kiska and ultimately to invade and capture the island. There was not much they could do to stop this unless they were willing to make a major fleet effort in the north. And in the south the Japanese were fighting the battles of the Solomons and New Guinea, which took most of their attention.

They decided that they would evacuate the Aleutians, using a new technique. Rather than sending destroyers to waters infested by American cruisers and battleships, they would use their big I-boats, the fleet-class submarines. So now, in the spring of 1943, the Japanese began sending in one I-boat on an average of every three days, to bring supplies to the garrison and evacuate key personnel.

The first was *I-7*, which came into Kiska on the night of May 26, even as the fighting still continued on Attu. She brought in food, weapons, and ammunition and took out 60 passengers. A few days later she came back and took out 101 men.

All during June the I-boats came and went, but not without some difficulties.

The guns had not yet stopped firing on May 29, 1943, when the army engineers landed and looked over the Japanese airfield at Holtz Bay and searched for other airfield sites on Attu. The navy also landed engineers on the flat island of Shemya, 25 miles east of Attu, to build a field suitable for B-29s. It appeared that the worst Japanese fears were to be realized and that the Aleutians would become the takeoff point for air raids against Japan.

Now the North Pacific Command began to consider the specific problems of assaulting Kiska. It would require many more troops and ships than the Attu attack, because the number of defenders on Kiska was estimated to be 10,000. General DeWitt that May organized an amphibious training force under General Corlett. Preliminary training was to be carried out at Fort Ord and the San Diego facility. The joint army-navy staff that had planned the Attu operation would be involved, but advanced training would also be given at Adak Island.

As a result of the experience gained on Attu, the size of the American force was more than doubled. Also other units were brought in: a mountain combat team, a regimental combat team from the Alaska Defense Command, and the First Special Service Force. About 600 men of the First Special Service Force were Canadians, and a Canadian Brigade was also included, numbering 4,800 officers and men. All of these units were specially trained in arctic warfare of the sort fought on Attu. The relief of the Seventeenth Infantry had been planned but since they were battle-tested, the high command decided to keep them. In July 1943, then, 34,000 troops were assembled at Adak and Amchitka islands for final training for the assault. Some of the army planners wanted to delay the assault on Kiska, but the American people were eager to see this threat to the United States and Canada eliminated, and so the Joint Chiefs of Staff gave approval to the Kiska attack plan on June 22. There was some argument again from the army about dates of actual operation, but Admiral Nimitz came down on the side of speedy action, and so the date for D-Day was set. It would be August 15, 1943.

Having inspected the Japanese airfield on Holtz Bay, the American engineers rejected it and chose instead a spot on the east side of Massacre Bay. By June 8 that field was finished and ready to take aircraft. By June 21 the Shemya field was suitable for medium bombers.

In May 1943 American submarines increased their watch on the Aleutians but the old S-boats that were in use did not manage to find many enemy vessels. The targets were so few in this area that Admiral Nimitz had long ago withdrawn all the fleet submarines for more productive patrols. However, on the morning of May 27 Lieutenant Commander Irvin S. Hartman had his *S-41* on her sixth patrol, off Paramushiro in the Kuriles, when he sighted a seaplane tender. The tender ran away from the S-boat, but soon the captain came upon a large sailing schooner. Skipper Hartman fired two torpedoes at the schooner; all four masts fell and she sank. On May 31 the *S-41* torpedoed a small freighter that contained some volatile materials, for it blew up with an enormous roar, sending debris and flames up a thousand feet into the sky.

The Japanese submarine evacuation of Kiska continued. The *I-24* made a successful round trip and then set out on another. But on this second voyage on June 10 she encountered the American patrol boat *PC-487*, under Lieutenant Wallace G. Cornell. The patrol boat picked up the submarine first by sonar, and then by radar in the fog. A few minutes after the radar contact the periscopes appeared, so the patrol boat closed in and dropped five depth charges. The submarine was blown upward and surfaced. The patrol boat rammed her and then rammed her again while firing three-inch and 20-mm guns. The submarine rolled over and sank.

The *I-9* was sunk by gunfire by the destroyer *Frazier* on June 13. The *I-31* was sunk, perhaps by one of the bombers. The *I-155* suffered hull damage in a storm and went home without delivering her supplies or picking up any men. The *I-2* and *I-157* had similar mishaps.

On June 11, also off Paramushiro, the *S-30* sank a 5,000-ton freighter, and the *S-35* sank a crab cannery ship off the coast of Kamchatka on June 12.

Shortly after the fall of Attu to the Americans, Admiral Kinkaid established a Kiska blockade and announced that the island would be bombed several times every day that weather permitted. The cruiser-destroyer force watched for the coming of the Japanese fleet, but it did not occur. Imperial General Headquarters decided after the fall of Attu that there was no point in engaging the North Pacific Force at the moment and disassembled the ship formations that had been made ready and sent most of them for training in the Inland Sea.

The Eleventh Air Force and the navy changed tactics for the air war. The Eleventh Air Force adopted a new slogan—"Never miss a break" and determined to bomb and strafe Kiska on every day they could fly. They increased their flying by working with navy Ventura bombers equipped with special radar to guide them to the target in fog. The first such cooperative raid was flown on June 4 when six B-24s of the 404th Bombardment Squadron followed a Ventura to make a radar-controlled bomb run over Kiska's North Head. Between June and August 15 the Eleventh Air Force made 1,454 sorties against Kiska and dropped 155 tons of bombs. A few planes were shot down by antiaircraft gunfire, but as usual up there most of the air force losses were operational. The navy Catalinas also participated, doing some night bombing of the island.

The Attu field was ready on June 8 and a C-47 transport landed there that day, bringing up fighter pilots. After that operations were curtailed for nearly two weeks by weather. On June 21 the new fighter strip on Shemya Island was ready although all missions in the area were canceled that day for the tenth straight day.

The Japanese were maintaining communication with Kiska by ship and submarine both.

On June 22 the *I-7* made her third round-trip to Kiska to unload supplies and take men home to Japan. She got into a fight with the destroyer *Monaghan* and was driven ashore, damaged. She was refloated in a few hours and tried to escape when three patrol boats attacked her and drove her ashore again. This time she was lost.

On June 22 a P-40 pilot on a mission to Kiska sighted a submarine near the island's Zeto Point, but when a B-24 went out to bomb the submarine it could not make contact. Most of the air attacks were made against the main camp area, although other installations were also hit. Sometimes the anti-aircraft guns seemed almost somnolent, and then sometimes they were fiercely active, as on July 2 when intensive fire damaged three B-25s. Several B-25s went after a submarine that day but did not hit it and dropped their bombs on the Kiska seaplane base instead.

The Americans were only dimly aware of the intensive nature of the Japanese submarine activity at Kiska those days. That spring and summer of 1942, after the fall of Attu, the Japanese I-boats had been coming into Kiska bringing supplies, continuing on an average of one every three days. For the most part they were undetected since they operated mostly at night. And when they were spotted, they dived as soon as they knew they were observed.

Toward the end of June Admiral Kawase, who was responsible for the evacuation of Kiska, totalled up his results. Seven of the 13 submarines he was using to evacuate the garrison had been lost or crippled and he had only taken out 820 men. He decided to cancel the submarine program.

On July 6 Rear Admiral Robert C. Giffen, in the cruiser *Wichita*, led a cruiser force of three heavy cruisers, one light cruiser, and four destroyers in a bombardment raid on Kiska, the ships firing several hundred shells into the island installations.

Another submarine was sighted on July 7, but when the B-25s involved went to make a bomb run, the submarine crash-dived and they saw no more of it. The next night the *Aylwin* and the *Monaghan* made a bombardment raid on Kiska. In fact in the next 20 days they bombarded Kiska five times.

On July 10 the Eleventh Air Force, for the first time since the Doolittle Tokyo raid, staged an attack on Japanese home territory. Eight B-25s bombed Paramushiro, shipping in

Paramushiro Strait, and Shimushu Island across the strait. The attacks were made through heavy cloud cover. There was no way of scoring the results. They saw no enemy aircraft and encountered no antiaircraft fire. They were supposed to be accompanied by B-24s but that raid was diverted at the last moment to be sent against a convoy spotted off Attu. The B-24s went in low and claimed to have sunk two Japanese freighters.

On July 11 the B-24s and B-25s returned to the Paramushiro area, but heavy weather prevented them from finding any of the shipping for which they were searching. They turned back without dropping their bombs.

On July 22 the battleships *Mississippi* and *New Mexico*, five cruisers, and nine destroyers, under Rear Admiral Robert M. Griffin, went to bombard Kiska, while Admiral Giffen with his three cruisers and one light cruiser made a second bombardment raid. The battleships bombarded Kiska Harbor while the cruiser force hit Little Kiska, South Head, and Gertrude Cove. The bombardment was followed up by air raids. Twenty P-38s strafed, and 10 B-25s bombed, with more American and Canadian fighters coming in to make strafing runs, too. One plane was lost. But as the Americans learned later from a Japanese diary, the Japanese were so well dug in that not one life was lost in what the diarist called "the most furious battle" of the campaign. One barracks was destroyed and two others were damaged. That was all.

The Japanese in Tokyo regarded this increase in air and naval activity as the prelude to American invasion of Kiska, and they had to make a decision. Should they repeat the story of Attu, with these thousands of soldiers? Or should they follow the Guadalcanal pattern, recognize that the Aleutians had become a lost cause, and evacuate the troops? With all those battleships and heavy cruisers about, it was evident that if Imperial Headquarters chose the latter course, they would have to use a new technique.

That was their decision. They would evacuate the troops. They knew that the job had to be done soon. The Americans were growing more belligerent all the time. On one day missions were flown against Kiska by 62 P-40s. On July

26 the Eleventh Air Force dropped 104 tons of bombs on Kiska, the highest one-day total yet for the Eleventh Air Force. Some of those planes bombed the submarine base, and they sighted two submarines in the area.

But the major evacuation of the Japanese on Kiska was under way, and it was not by submarine. On July 21, under the cover of thick weather all over the region, Rear Admiral Masatomi Kimura, the commander of Destroyer Squadron One, set out from Paramushiro with two light cruisers and 10 destroyers for Kiska. Behind came the tanker *Nippon Maru* and the escort vessel *Kunashiro*. Admiral Kawase accompanied the evacuation force in the light cruiser *Tama*.

On July 25 the Japanese force arrived at a point 500 miles southwest of Kiska. There the destroyers fueled and made preparations for their dash in and out. The fog was so dense that the Americans were not searching out that way, although they bombed Kiska. The fog was so dense, in fact, that two of Admiral Kimura's ships collided, although the damage done was not too serious.

At noon on July 28 the evacuation group started their final run to Kiska through the fog. By 6:30 that evening they were anchoring in the harbor, which was completely fogged over. The soldiers had been preparing to leave all day long, setting demolition charges and booby traps. The Japanese set fire to the barracks and supply huts, blew the demolition charges, and assembled on the shore, taking only a few personal belongings. In an hour the boats had taken them all onto the destroyers and cruisers. Finally more than 5,000 men were jammed aboard the ships, and they were ready to sail. The fog lifted just then, and they left the harbor in clear weather and steamed south to rejoin Admiral Kawase and the support forces. The ships reached Paramushiro on July 31 without incident. For the second time within a year, the Japanese had managed so skillful an evacuation that the Americans knew nothing about it.

CHAPTER TWENTY-FOUR

The Invasion of Kiska

If the Americans were blockading Kiska as they said they were, they were doing a very bad job of it. As the Japanese cruiser and destroyers headed out of the harbor, they found themselves absolutely alone on the sea. No night-flying PBYs were overhead or came to take a look. No American destroyers were on station doing their blockade duty. The Americans were as soundly asleep as they had been at the time of the Pearl Harbor attack.

The reason was that somebody was seeing things.

On July 23, 1943, five days before the destroyer evacuation of Kiska, a PBY on patrol "saw" a convoy of ships 200 miles southwest of Attu. If they were ships they might have been Soviet fishing vessels. But probably they were not even that, but products of the tricks played so often on the minds of the Americans in the Aleutians: low-lying clouds, shadows and mist, or a school of whales. The PBY crew did not actually see anything; they picked up seven blips on their search radar.

At the headquarters of the Northwest Pacific Command this report received complete credence. It was just what Admiral Kinkaid and his staff were looking for. Knowing nothing about the earlier start of the Japanese evacuation by submarine, they assumed that the Japanese on Kiska would behave as had the Japanese on Attu and prepare to defend their conquest to the last man. Admiral Kinkaid called his two task forces and alerted them to the danger. The two blockading destroyers, the *Aylwin* and the *Monaghan*, were pulled off station and told to join up with the task forces and go out and fight the Japanese convoy that the PBY had snooped.

On the night of July 25 Admiral Giffen formed up his bombardment battleship, cruiser, and destroyer force 80 miles southwest of Kiska and started west to intercept the reported convoy. It was a clear night and the moon was shining for a welcome change. Soon the battleship *Mississippi*'s radar operator reported contacts on the port bow, out only 15 miles. The operators of the *Portland, Wichita,* and *Idaho* also said they saw them. The ships all went to general quarters and prepared for a battle. When the blips were eight miles away, Admiral Giffen altered course to evade torpedoes and just after midnight began firing at the "blips." The destroyers were sent off to make torpedo attacks of their own. The radar operators kept feeding information to the gunners about the movement of the enemy force. The lookouts reported seeing torpedo wakes passing close by. The crew felt concussion of the sort that should come from near misses. (Having never been in battle, it is remarkable that they knew.) Gunners reported star shell illumination by the enemy. One sailor collapsed from battle fatigue, or shell shock as they used to call it. Altogether it was a stirring battle, except that "the enemy" did not fire back, and the cruiser *San Francisco* and the destroyers could not find anything at all on their radar screens.

Half an hour after the battle began, Admiral Giffen began to smell a mouse. They must have sunk all those ships because the radar screens were suddenly as clear as glass. Nothing showed. He ordered the ships to cease firing. The ships had fired a thousand rounds. They headed into the area where the ships were supposed to be and found nothing. When dawn came the admiral sent up spotter planes, and they found nothing. The admiral and his staff concluded that what they had seen on the radar were return echoes from the mountains of Amchitka and the other western Aleutian islands.

So the battle of the pips ended and the Americans retired muttering. Meanwhile the Japanese destroyers waited 500 miles from Kiska and when the weather was sufficiently soupy they made their run into Kiska. By that time Admiral

Giffen was fueling his ships from a tanker a hundred miles southeast of Kiska and the sea was wide open for the Japanese and the skies were hanging on top of the water.

July 28, the day the Japanese destroyer evacuation force sailed from Kiska, the weather over the island was too foggy for air operations and all missions were scrubbed. On July 29 one lone B-17 scouted the main camp area and bombed but received no return fire. On July 30 the destroyers *Farragut* and *Hull* were on blockade station, guarding the empty island. They fired 200 rounds of five-inch ammunition at the buildings. On August 1 seven B-24s flew over Kiska and bombed through the heavy overcast. On August 2 two battleships, two heavy cruisers, three light cruisers, and nine destroyers fired 2,300 shells at the island and received no return fire. The air force also was seeing things. On August 2 two "enemy" planes were picked up over Attu but when fighters went up to attack them, there was nothing to see.

The air force attacked again on August 3. On August 4 the Eleventh Air Force boasted that it dropped 153 tons of bombs on Kiska, a new record for the Aleutians. Reconnaissance planes reported fires started in the main camp area, and on Little Kiska. Later in the day 86 bombers and 80 fighters attacked, bombing and strafing the radio station, the gun batteries, and buildings.

That day Admiral Kinkaid's intelligence officer sent a memorandum to the admiral, including a sheaf of photographs that had been taken by reconnaissance planes on August 2.

"Never before since the original occupation of Kiska has so much destruction been created in an equivalent period of time," the memo said. "Twenty-six buildings had been destroyed, including the radio stations, garages, storage buildings, and barracks. Of 20 barges seen in the harbor a week earlier, only one remained. The bombardment men and the air force must be congratulated on having done such a superb job of destruction." But there were a few strange little things.

Previously the Japanese had been meticulous about concealing and camouflaging their motor vehicles. But here they were all parked down near the shore neatly as if in a motor pool.

The Japanese must have been woefully short of ammunition, because in the past week not one shot had been fired by the artillery on the bombarding destroyers. But the air force reported "light flak" had been fired from time to time against the aircraft that attacked the island. One pilot reported seeing tracers fired up at him as he strafed. Another pilot said he had strafed a Japanese soldier and had seen the man fall flat.

But why had Radio Kiska gone off the air on July 28? Nothing had been heard from it since, even before the radio building was destroyed, and no apparent attempt to make repairs had been noted.

General Howland Smith suggested that the way to find out what was going on would be to send scouts to the island in rubber boats and take a look. Admiral Kinkaid heard the suggestion but rejected it. The reconnaissance party might be wiped out, he said. If the Japanese were still on the island, the troops and ships would be ready for them. If there were no Japanese there, it would be a superb rehearsal for an amphibious landing, a great training program.

Someone on the staff suggested that perhaps the Japanese had evacuated the island using all those submarines that had been noticed a month or so earlier.

Admiral Kinkaid laughed and said he would be glad to provide transportation for the garrison. He was sure the Japanese had taken to the hills and were digging in for an Attu sort of last stand. That day more photo missions were flown, and the next and the next. More bombing and strafing raids were made and the destruction continued, but no return fire came up. Obviously the Japanese were up to something, and Admiral Kinkaid suspected it was trickery. The Japanese might be hoarding their ammunition and lying low, waiting for the invasion attempt. So the bombing and strafing continued and the photo missions continued and the preparations for the invasion continued.

Major General Charles H. Corlett commanded 34,000 troops, more than 5,000 of them Canadian. General DeWitt and General Howland Smith came up to Adak, and John J.

McCloy, the Assistant Secretary of War, came up too, to observe the show.

More than a hundred ships assembled in the harbor at Adak. The soldiers spent several days on that island practicing marching and moving about on the soggy tundra. Then on Friday, August 13, 1943, the expedition sailed from Adak.

The first ships arrived at Kiska on August 15. The minesweepers went in first to clear the areas where the transports would anchor, southwest of Gertrude Cove. The battleships, cruisers, and destroyers fired bombardment at the Japanese camps. Five strange boats left the transport area and sped into the shore, loaded with troops. But they did not land. The troops were wooden dummies and the boats were disguised PT boats. The purpose of the exercise was to draw Japanese fire and expose any trickery that was about to occur and to convince the Japanese that the main landings would be at Gertrude Cove. Meanwhile the real landing force was aboard LSTs, LCIs and LCTs and they moved onto the beach midway up the western side of the island. Soon 7,300 soldiers were ashore, looking for the enemy. They searched and searched, but they did not draw any fire. They bedded down for the night fearful of a banzai attack. There was no attack, no sign of any Japanese.

On the morning of August 16 the transports landed more troops four miles south of Kiska Volcano. American and Canadian patrols fanned out across the island and occupied Gertrude Cove. Occasionally the patrolling soldiers would hear gunfire but they did not encounter any Japanese. In fact, the Allied troops were firing at one another, and although there were no Japanese on the island, the Allies suffered casualties—21 men killed and 121 wounded.

On August 17 the soldiers reached the Japanese main camp, and there they saw the signs of a hasty evacuation of the camp. Much food, supplies, and weapons had not been destroyed. Still, that did not mean that the Japanese were not lurking up on the sides of the mountains, and the soldiers continued to search and to fire on one another.

On August 18 a Japanese mine broke loose from its mooring and drifted against the destroyer *Abner Read* when she was making a night patrol off the beach. An explosion blew apart the ship's stern. A ruptured smoke tank began pouring out smoke into the ship, and the smoke paralyzed the respiratory muscles of trapped crewmen who died from smoke inhalation. Finally the stern broke off near the after gun mount and many men were carried down into the icy water. Some were saved by the ship's boats, but many men drowned. The *Abner Read* lost 70 men dead or missing and 47 wounded. The destroyer *Bancroft* towed the *Abner Read* to Adak.

For five more days, from August 18 to August 22, the soldiers continued to search for the enemy. For a little while the commanders thought they might have the answer. From Washington came a message that a doctor who had lived on Kiska for a time in 1902 remembered that there were several large caves on the island, each capable of holding a thousand men.

Was that where the Japanese had gone? The search began, but no Japanese were found, in or out of caves. The only living things were four mongrel dogs.

One embryo Byron put together the general feeling of the soldiers in verse:

Tales of Kiska

"You've heard the bloody tales of old,
Of fearless knights and warriors bold,
But now the muse pens tales of Kiska,
Or how we missed them by a whisker.

"One hundred thousand men at muster,
Admirals, generals, adding lustre;
Two hundred planes, as many ships,
All were bound for Kiska's Nips.
And now we come to how and when
'Dog-day' got its cognomen.

"Dog-day's evening found our log
Quoting the capture of one dog.

"Dog-day plus one and two and three
Found three more in captivity.
But as for Japs, we couldn't say
We've seen one, either night or day.

"We searched volcanic craters vast
To catch a glimpse of one at last.
It took three days before we learnt
That more than dogs there simply weren't.

"O, here's to mighty ComNorPac
Whose kingdom lay at cold Adak.
Whose reign was known in fame for fog
And capture of two couple dog."

The whole story of the invasion of Kiska made the front pages of American newspapers and was copied abroad by the neutral press, and the story was told by radio. The Japanese soon had the story and the knowledge that their thousands of men from Kiska were safe in the Kuriles.

A hundred thousand men, an armada of ships, a whole air force had been tied up for a year in these islands. In the height of the excitement the air force had dropped a hundred thousand leaflets on the island, calling on the Japanese to surrender.

"The only problem," said one airman, "was that those dogs couldn't read."

CHAPTER TWENTY-FIVE

Exit the Aleutians

In August 1943 the Alaskans, the Canadians, and the Americans celebrated the reconquest of the Aleutians. The Japanese, when they stopped congratulating themselves on their successful evacuation, could then count the cost of the misadventure that had been a part of the whole miscarried Midway plan. They had lost three destroyers, six submarines, and nine cargo ships in reinforcing Attu and Kiska. One whole garrison at Adak had been sacrificed almost to a man. The Eleventh Air Force had destroyed 69 aircraft and also claimed to have sunk 21 ships and damaged another 29 ships while losing 29 of its own aircraft. The navy had lost a number of PBYs, almost all of them to weather.

The Japanese reaction to the fall of their Aleutians bases was to abolish the Northern Area Force and combine the Fifth Fleet and the Twelfth Air Fleet as the Twelfth Area Fleet, which would be based at Paramushiro and Ominato for the defense of the Kuriles. The naval components of the force were one heavy cruiser, two light cruisers, two destroyer divisions, seven transports, and a number of smaller service craft. This was considered adequate for defense, and there would be no more adventures in the north.

Now that the Allies had recovered the Aleutians, what would they do? Would they use the Aleutians for air bases from which to bomb Adak's long airstrip that had been built with an eye to its use by B-29s for just such a purpose? One thing the Aleutian campaign had taught the air force was that it did not want to operate aircraft any more than it had to in this foggy, stormy climate.

And what about using the Aleutians as a base for the invasion of the Kurile Islands?

Early in August, before the invasion of Kiska, General DeWitt had submitted such a plan to General George C. Marshall, the army chief of staff. After all, there were 140,000 men now in this area, and would it not be sensible to make use of them? The combined forces that had been involved in the Attu and Kiska operations numbered 54,000 men. The general proposed the organization of a North American Theater to carry out the invasion of the Kuriles, and to do it in April or May 1944.

But in Washington the DeWitt plan was met with skepticism. The navy was fully committed to the operations in the Central and South Pacific. Upcoming were the Gilberts invasion and Admiral Halsey's invasion of Empress Augusta Bay in Bougainville, and after that the navy looked to the Marshalls and the Marianas. General Marshall was committed to the operations of General MacArthur in the Southwest Pacific. So neither the navy nor the army high commands looked with favor on the creation of a North American Theater.

Also, what would be gained by an invasion of Paramushiro and the other Kurile Islands? Would not the United States be likely to find itself in the position of the Japanese in reverse? Would they not have to expend enormous resources to supply and maintain a garrison in conditions almost like those of the Aleutians while the Japanese could easily attack them with air and naval forces from the home islands?

The project was discussed by the Joint Chiefs of Staff on September 7, which referred it to their planning committee. The committee talked to Admiral Nimitz, Admiral Kinkaid, and General DeWitt, and on September 18 came up with a negative recommendation. Such a plan would make sense only if it was to be followed by an invasion of Hokkaido. The British and American Combined Chiefs of Staff had considered this already and rejected it. There were much better approaches to Japan than that from the north. And in 1943 with the war in Europe still gaining momentum, the date for an invasion of Japan seemed a long way off.

Further, the army and navy had already begun to disassemble the forces in the north. Admiral Kinkaid left the North Pacific Command in October 1943 to go to the Southwest Pacific and take over General MacArthur's navy, which was named the Seventh Fleet. That fleet needed vessels desperately if it was to mount the offensive operations the Joint Chiefs of Staff called for in the Southwest Pacific, up the shore of New Guinea, heading toward the Philippines.

Admiral Kinkaid was replaced as commander of the Northern command by Vice Admiral Frank Jack Fletcher, whose showing as a carrier commander, particularly at the invasion of Guadalcanal, had convinced Admiral King that Fletcher needed to go ashore.

The Eleventh Air Force was whittled down by the dispatch of several of its heavy bombardment and medium bombardment squadrons back to the continental United States. They could be much more profitably employed in other theaters. American military commanders in England, Italy, and the Central and South Pacific were all clamoring for more air power, and the battle of the Atlantic against the German submarines was far from over. There was one possibility. If Russia entered the war against Japan, then it could make sense to invade the Kuriles in conjunction with the Russians. This project was discussed and approved tentatively, and it was decided that the Western Aleutians would not be stripped of defenses but gradually strengthened again to that end. It seemed to be a long way off. A tentative date for planning the invasion of the Kuriles under these conditions was set for the spring of 1945.

In the fall, the Eleventh Air Force made a series of raids on the Kuriles but they had to be minimal because the air force had been cut back, to 16 medium bombers, 12 heavy bombers, and 100 fighters. The raids were largely in retaliation for Japanese air raids on the Aleutians, as on October 9 when a dozen Kurile-based Japanese bombers attacked Attu, and on October 13 when eight medium bombers attacked around Massacre Bay. But by the end of 1943, the threat of Japan against the Aleutians and Alaska was over, and in 1944 the Aleutians and Alaskan garrisons were reduced to 50,000 men.

NOTES

1 Preparing For War

The letter to Franklin D. Roosevelt is in the FDR papers in Hyde Park, New York. The material about the American attitude in the 1930s is from studies made for my *The Tempering Years*. The material about continental defenses is from the Conn book, *Guarding the United States and its Outposts*. The discussion on naval maneuvers is from Morison's *The Rising Sun in the Pacific*. The material about Japanese language officers is from *And I Was There*, the memoirs of Admiral E. T. Layton. The material about the naval treaties is from studies made for my *Yamamoto*. The material about the Hepburn report is from the Morison book, hereafter called *Rising Sun*.

2 Defense of Hawaii

The material about the Treaty of Portsmouth is from materials gathered for my *Pacific Destiny*. The army mission is defined in Conn. The preoccupation of the army with sabotage more than enemy attack is a phenomenon stemming from American anti-Japanese feelings of the time. The Markham report is detailed in Conn. The material about the fleet changes is from *Rising Sun*. The discussion of General Marshall's views is from Conn, as is the discussion of General Short's actions. The material about Japanese-American relations is from materials collected for my *Japan's War*. The story of the Short-Bloch meeting is from Conn. The material about the Honolulu newspapers is from the pages of the *Honolulu Advertiser*. The material about the imposition of martial law in Hawaii is from Conn. To my mind martial law was as cruel and unnecessary as the evacuation of the Japanese from the West Coast, and the responsibility for it lies with President Roosevelt, who heartily approved both measures.

3 The Western Perimeter

The material about the Japanese submarines in Hawaii waters is from Conn. The story of the Japanese attack on the Philippines is from the archives of the MacArthur Memorial Museum in Norfolk. The story of the attack on Guam is from *Rising Sun*. The story of the defense of Wake Island is from *Rising Sun*. The material about Admiral Kimmel and his plans comes from the files of the Navy Operational Archives in Washington. The story of Admiral Pye's indecisiveness and the Wake Island relief expedition is from materials in the Operational Archives and from an interview with Admiral Milo F. Draemel who was Pye's chief of staff. My appraisal of Admiral Fletcher is made after studying all his carrier battles from reports in the Operational Archives. The story of the *Ward* and the *Antares* is from a combat narrative by the *Ward*'s captain, in the Operational Archives.

4 Against Sabatoge and Espionage

The story of the army actions in Hawaii is from Conn.

5 West Coast Defense

The discussion of the West Coast defenses is from Conn and *Rising Sun*. The false tale about the 20,000 Japanese in San Francisco who were ready to riot is from Conn.

6 The Decision

The discussion of Yamamoto's plans comes from materials collected for my *Yamamoto*.

7 Striking the American Perimeter in the South

The study of the Japanese plans comes from studies made for my *Japan's War* and my *Japan's Triumph*. The story of the battle of the Coral Sea is from the Navy Operational Archives ship's action reports.

8 First Midway, Then Hawaii

The material about Japanese staff officers and their studies comes from a conversation with Captain Shin Itonaga of the Japanese Self Defense Force. The story of Nimitz's plans for Midway is from Admiral Layton's book. The story of the battle of Midway is from *Rising Sun* and the CinCPac War Diary in the Operational Archives.

9 Alaskan Defenses

The material about the prewar defenses in Alaska is from Conn and *Rising Sun*.

10 When the Japanese Came

The material about the Japanese reaction to the Doolittle raid is from my *Yamamoto*. The material about Admiral King is from my *Nimitz and His Admirals*. The material about Alaskan defenses is from Conn. The material about Admiral Theobald is from *Rising Sun*. The material about the army air force activities is from the Carter chronology of air force operations.

11 The Japanese Attack

The material about the Japanese plan for the Aleutians and Midway is from the *Boei Sensshi Shitsu* (War History), 101 volumes, Midway Operations (*Midowai Sakusen*). The material about the attack is from Midway Operations and *Rising Sun*.

12 Arctic War

The stories of American submarines in the Aleutians are from the submarine patrol reports in the navy's Operational

Archives. The stories of the air attacks on the Aleutians are from Carter.

13 Problems of Command

The stories of the air force are from Carter. The material about War Department operations is from Conn. The material about Admiral Theobald's operations is from Morison's *Aleutians, Gilberts and Marshalls*, hereafter called *Aleutians*. Morison does not go into much detail about the constant bickering between army and navy commands in the Aleutians, but the fact is that Admiral Theobald was relieved of command because of it and Admiral Kinkaid came in.

14 The Japanese Problem

The description of Kiska is from *Aleutians*, as is the material about naval operations. Carter is the source of the stories of the air force.

15 Enter Admiral Kinkaid

The material about Admiral Kinkaid's operations is from a long interview with Kinkaid in 1968 and from *Aleutians*. The stories of the air force operations are from Carter. The story of Admiral McMorris's activities is from the Operational Archives, Northern Command War Diary and ships' action reports.

16 Wearing Down the Enemy

The story of the plans for the invasion of Attu are from *Aleutians*, and Conn. The stories of the air activities are from Carter.

17 The Battle of the Komandorski Islands

The story of the battle of the Komandorski Islands is from *Aleutians* and the ships' action reports.

18 Attu

The material about Attu is from *Aleutians* and Conn. The story of the invasion is from Conn.

19 The Landings on Attu

The story of the landings on Attu is from Conn and *Aleutians*. The story of air activity is from Carter.

20–21–22

The story of the battle for Attu is from Conn. The story of the relief of General Brown is from Conn and *Aleutians*.

23–24

The story of the battle for Kiska is from Conn, *Aleutians*, and Carter.

25 Exit the Aleutians

The material about the DeWitt plan is from Conn. The material about Frank Jack Fletcher and Kinkaid is from *Aleutians*, and from Admiral Nimitz's correspondence file.

BIBLIOGRAPHY

Carter, Kit C., and Robert Mueller. *The Army Air Forces in World War II, Combat Chronology*. Washington, D. C.: Office of Air Force History, Headquarters, USAF, 1973.

Conn, Stetson, Rose C. Engelman, and Byron Fairchild. *Guarding the United States and Its Outposts*. Washington, D. C.: Office of Military History, U.S. Army. Undated.

Morison, Samuel Eliot. *The Rising Sun in the Pacific*. Boston: Atlantic-Little Brown, 1948.

Aleutians, Gilberts and Marshalls. Boston: Atlantic-Little Brown, 1951.

INDEX

Abner Read, 164–165
Abukuma, 116, 120
Adak Island, 82–83, 84, 95, 96–97, 99, 104, 105, 108, 116, 120, 126, 130, 147, 154; American occupation of, 104; American troops landing on, 97; Japanese plan to strike, 82, 85; Theobald's decision to build airfield on, 96–97
Agano, 137
Aggatu Island, 90
Akagane Maru, 110
Akagi, 71
Akebono Maru, 67
Alaska, 9, 10, 12, 13, 55, 63, 73–76, 78, 89, 93, 128; celebrating reconquest of Aleutians, 167; defenses, 73–76, 78, 80; railroads in, 74
Alaskan Defense Command (U.S.), 74, 93, 154
Alaska Scout Detachment (U.S.), 136
Amchitka Island, 89, 96, 98, 99, 101, 106, 107, 109, 113, 114, 116, 138, 154
American-Canadian Permanent Joint Board on Defense, 4, 5
American Samoa, 45, 58, 78
Antares, 38
Arare, 90
Arctic war, 89–91
Argentina Maru, 89

Asaka Maru, 116
Asiatic Fleet (U.S.), 10
Astoria, 37, 71
Atka Island, 87, 103; Americans building air strip on, 106
Atlantic Fleet (U.S.), 25
Attu Island, 77, 80, 83, 87, 94, 98–99, 100, 102, 110–111, 112, 114, 117, 127–151, 152, 154, 168; American troops landing on, 134–141; banzi attack by Japanese, 150–151; description of, 128–129; fall of, 147–151; fight for, 142–146; Guadalcanal-style effort to resupply Attu by Japanese, 133; Japanese building air strip on, 109; Japanese occupation of, 87; Japanese troops on, 129; Japanese withdrawal toward Chichagof Harbor, 147; missionaries on, 79; Operation Landgrab, 130
Australia, 57, 59
Aylwin, 157, 160

Bailey, 118, 119, 123, 125, 126; attack on, 125–126
B-17 aircraft, 17, 18, 20, 21, 22, 23, 24, 63, 66, 67–68, 69, 75, 78, 80, 84, 92, 93, 94
B-24 aircraft, 92, 93, 94, 97–

177

B-24 aircraft (*cont.*)
98, 99, 107, 108, 112, 114,
116, 134, 135, 142, 145,
149, 156, 157, 158, 162
B-25 aircraft, 107, 108, 112,
114, 116, 126, 134, 142,
150, 157, 158
B-26 aircraft, 63, 84, 100,
107, 108
B-29 aircraft, 54, 167
Battle of Coral Sea, 61, 63, 64
Battle of Komandorski
Islands, 118–127, 129, 132
Betty bombers, 149
Bloch, Claude, 23
Brown, Albert E., 113, 130,
141, 142–148; Rockwell,
conference with, 144
Brown, Wilson, 36, 37, 38,
39, 42, 44
Buckner, Simon Bolivar, 74,
80, 93, 95, 96, 97, 99,
101, 115, 141, 144, 148;
personality clash between
Theobald and, 100
Butler, General, 80, 95, 120

Canada, 3, 154; American-
Canadian Permanent Joint
Board on Defense, 4, 5;
celebrating reconquest of
Aleutians, 167; imprisoning
Japanese in camps, 53
Casco, 148
Catalina flying boats, 75, 80,
83, 90, 96, 103, 148, 156
Charleston, 74, 148, 149
Cheribon Maru, 105
Chikuma, 39, 137
China, 2, 3, 4, 8, 9, 23, 74
China Clipper, 32–33
Chiyoda, 89
Churchill, Winston, 57

Coghlan, 110, 118, 119, 123,
125, 133
Combined Fleet (Japan), 56,
59, 64, 66, 85, 135;
proposal to invade Hawaii,
61
Coral Sea, battle of, 61, 63,
64
Corlett, Charles H., 113, 154,
163
Cornell, Wallace G., 155
Cullin, Frank L., 136, 147
Cunningham, Commander,
41, 43, 44; unconditional
surrender to Japanese on
Wake Island, 45

Dale, 118, 119, 125
Denmark, 4–5
Detroit, 105, 132
Devereux, James P., 32, 33–
36, 44; unconditional
surrender to Japanese on
Wake Island, 45
Dewey, 107, 146
DeWitt, John L., 10, 93, 97,
101, 110–112, 113, 130,
144, 148, 154, 163, 168;
planning for invasion of
Kiska, 113
Doolittle, Jimmy, 56
Doolittle raid, 62, 77, 79, 157
Draemel, Milo F., 43
Drum, Hugh A., 16, 17
Dutch East Indies, 8
Dutch Harbor, 73, 74, 78–79,
80, 81, 84, 84–85, 86, 93,
101, 126; Japanese plan to
strike, 82

Earle, Edward P., 142
Edwards, 145
Eisenhower, Milton S., 53

Eleventh Air Force (U.S.),
74, 91, 92, 93, 107, 108,
113, 114, 116, 120, 134,
138, 142, 147–150, 156,
159, 162, 167, 169;
bombing of Kiska, 92;
bombing Paramushiro, 157–
158; increasing attacks on
Kiska and Attu islands,
118; strengthening of, 93
Eleventh Bomber Command
(U.S.), 116
Emmons, Delos C., 46, 49
England: *See* Great Britain
Enterprise, 24, 36, 64, 67,
70–71, 72, 86

Farragut, 145, 162
F4F Wildcat Fighters, 33
Fifth Fleet (Japan), 151, 167
Fiji Islands, 78
First Battalion (U.S.), 143
First Special Service Force
(Canada), 154
Fish, James, 150
Fitch, Aubrey W., 36, 37, 44
Fletcher, Frank Jack, 37, 39,
40–41, 43, 44, 67, 70, 71,
169
Fourth Fleet (Japan), 31, 32,
34
Fourth Infantry (U.S.), 130,
144
404th Heavy Bombardment
Squadron (U.S.), 96, 99,
156
501st Antiaircraft Battalion
(U.S.), 144
France, 3, 4; fall of, 6
Franklin Bell, 136
Frazier, 155
French Frigate Shoals, 49, 63,
65

Germany, 2–6, 11, 153;
influence in Latin America,
3; Rome-Berlin-Tokyo
alliance, 3
Giffen, Robert C., 157, 158,
161–162
Gilbert Islands, 38, 63
Gillespie, 110
Gillis, 83, 87, 91
Gilmore, Howard W., 89
Great Britain, 3–7; Royal
Navy, 5
Great Sitkin Island, 106, 108
Griffen, Robert M., 158
Growler, 89; attack on, 90
Gruening, Ernest, 101
Grumman Wildcat fighters, 32
Guadalcanal, 63, 95, 96, 104,
105, 107–108, 110, 115,
169; American invasion of,
103
Guadalupe, 91
Guam, 3, 10, 12–13, 29–30,
32, 34, 45, 62; Chamorro
Insular Force, 30–31;
Japanese attack on, 30;
location of, 31

Haquro, 137
Hainan Island, Japanese
occupation of, 74
Halsey, William F., 24, 36,
37, 39, 64, 115, 168
Hamilton, J. H., 33
Hammann, 72
Hartl, Albert E., 141
Hartman, Irvin S., 155
Haruna, 137
Hatsushimo, 116, 120, 125
Hawaii, 3, 5, 10, 28–29, 45,
46–49, 55, 61–72; defense
of, 14–27; emergency act
(M-Day Act), 25;

Hawaii (*cont.*)
evacuation of all Japanese,
46; Hawaii Division, 16;
Hickam Field, 16, 19;
Honolulu Advertiser, 24;
Japanese living in, U.S.
army's fear of sabotage and
espionage from, 15–16, 25–
26, 46–49; martial law,
under, 25–26, 46; M-Day
Act, 25; military censorship
of mail, 27; Oahu, 16–17;
Pearl Harbor, 10, 12, 15,
17, 22, 24–27, 32, 43, 50,
53; Wheeler Field, 16, 19
Herron, Charles D., 16, 19
Hiryu, 39, 71–72; attack on,
72
*History of U.S. Naval
Operations in World War II*
(Morison), 102
Hitler, Adolf, 2, 9, 18, 57
Hiyo, 137
Holtz Bay, 128–131
Honolulu, 75, 104
Honolulu Advertiser, 24
Hornet, 67, 70, 72, 86
Hosogaya, Boshiro, 55, 82,
85, 87, 96, 103, 106, 108,
114, 116, 119–122, 125,
127; conduct of battle of
Komandorski Islands,
Japan's views on, 127;
resupply mission to
Aleutians, 116–117, 118;
retirement, 127
Hull, 162
Hull, Cordell, 2
Hyate, 35

I-2, 155
I-7, 28, 153, 156
I-8, 51
I-9, 155

I-17, 51
I-24, 155
I-26, 77
I-31, 155
I-155, 155
I-157, 155
I-168, 72
Idaho, 131, 161
Ikazuchi, 116
Inazuma, 116
Indianapolis, 75, 107, 110,
118
Indochina, Japanese occupation
of northern, 7, 74
Inouye, Shigeyoshi, 32, 39
Italy, 2; Rome-Berlin-Tokyo
alliance, 3

J. Franklin Bell, 146
Japan, 6, 28–45, 54–56, 102–
105, 108–111; Aleutians,
plan for invasion of, 77–88;
Attu Island, Japanese
General Staff's decision to
abandon, 102; Bushido,
153; code of conduct to
guide Imperial Army, 153;
defense perimeter, 78, 107;
evacuation Aleutians, 153–
154; Guam, attack on, 30;
Imperial Army, 54, 57,
153; Imperial General
Headquarters, 28, 57, 58,
62, 86, 104–105, 107–108,
148, 151, 156, 158;
Imperial Navy, 82, 86;
invasion of Wake Island,
34, 41; naval officers
studying in U.S., 11;
occupation of Indochina,
U.S. response to, 7;
organizing Aleutians
invasion force, 82; *Panay*
incident, 3; Pearl Harbor,

attack on, 24–25, 32;
Philippines, assault on, 29;
Radio Tokyo, 127; Rome-
Berlin-Tokyo alliance, 3;
sanctions against, 22;
shipbuilding program, 11;
shipping shortage, 79;
striking American perimeter
in south, plans for, 57–72;
taking possession of Wake
Island, 45; Treaty of
Portsmouth, 14; U.S.
decision to avoid war with,
7
Jones, Lloyd E., 107
Jones, Mr. and Mrs. Charles,
79; capture by Japanese, 86
Junyo, 82, 83, 84, 87, 89

Kachosan Maru, 105
Kaqa, 71
Kajioka, Admiral, 35, 37, 39,
40
Kakuta, Admiral, 65, 82–85,
86
Kamikawa Maru, 91
Kane, 135
Kasumi, 90
Kawanishi flying boats, 49,
61, 87, 95, 98, 102
Kawase, Admiral, 132, 137,
148, 151, 157, 159
Keizan Maru, 104–105;
sinking of, 105
Kimikawa Maru, 134, 137,
148
Kimmel, Husband E., 10, 23,
27, 31–32, 36–39, 40, 44,
106; as commander of
Pacific Fleet, 20; difference
between Pye and, 42;
recommendations for strong
defensive Wake Island, 31,

36; Roosevelt ordering
removal of, 42
Kimura, Masatomi, 159
King, Ernest J., 59, 64, 73,
75, 77, 79, 93, 95, 96,
115, 120
Kinkaid, Thomas C., 101,
106–112, 123, 144–145,
148, 160, 162, 163, 168,
169; commanding Attu
operation, 130; decision to
invade Attu Island, 110–
111, 115; Kiska blockade,
establishing, 156; taking
command of naval forces,
106
Kirkpatrick, C. C., 90
Kisaragi, 35
Kiska Island, 63, 79, 80, 82–
83, 86, 89, 93, 94, 95, 98–
99, 100, 102, 104–105,
106, 108–116, 120, 131–
132, 135, 152–166, 168;
American-Canadian air
force group striking, 98;
battle for, 152–159;
bombing of by U.S., 90–
91, 92, 94, 97; evacuation
of Japanese on, 159;
invasion of, 160–166;
Japanese occupation of, 87;
size of, 102; "Tales of
Kiska" (Byron), 165–166
Knox, Frank, 46–47, 48;
pressing for evacuation of
Japanese in Hawaii, 46–48
Kodiak Island, 73, 74, 75,
78, 85, 91, 95
Koga, Admiral, 135, 137, 148
Komandorski Islands, battle
of, 118–127, 129, 132
Kondo, Nobutake, 55, 72
Kongo, 137
Kotohiro Maru, 107

Kumano, 137
Kunashiro, 159
Kurile Islands, 168, 169
Kwajalein Island, 152

Landrum, Eugene L., 113, 146, 147; relieving Brown as commander of ground forces, 146
League of Nations, 3
Lexington, 36, 37, 38, 39, 59; sinking of, 64
London Naval Agreement of 1934, 73
Louisville, 104
Lukes, H. L., 89

MacArthur, Douglas, 23, 115, 168, 169; retreat into Bataan Peninsula, 29
MacDonough, 135
Malaya, 4
Manchuria, 23
Marine Fighter Squadron 222 (U.S.), 36
Marine Fighter Squadron VMF-211 (U.S.), 32, 40
Marine First Defense Battalion (U.S.), 32
Markham, Edward M., 17–18, 22; prediction regarding war with Japan, 17
Marre Island, 126
Marshall, George C., 15, 19, 20–21, 22, 23, 25, 79, 93, 97, 99, 101, 168
Marshall Islands, 31, 63
Martinez, Joe P., 152
Massacre Bay, 129–131
Maya, 116, 119, 121, 122, 123, 124, 137
McCloy, John J., 47, 163–164
McMillin, G. J., 30

McMorris, Charles H., 23, 43, 106, 107, 109–110, 118–121, 123–126, 132–133
Midway Island, 3, 10, 12, 13, 22, 23, 31, 32, 45, 54, 55, 56, 59, 61–72, 77, 79; attack on, 68–72; battle of Midway, 85; Japanese movement toward, 65
Midway Occupation Force (Japan), 66
Minneapolis, 37
Mississippi, 158, 161
Mitchell, Billy, 73
Mogami, 137
Monaghan, 91, 118, 119, 125, 156–157, 160
Monroe Doctrine, 4
Montreal Maru, 107
Morison, Samuel Eliot, 13, 42, 102
Musashi, 11; 137
Mussolini, Benito, 2
Myoko, 137

Nachi, 82, 116, 119, 121, 122, 123, 124, 125; attack on, 121, 122, 125
Nagara, 71
Nagumo, Chuichi, 39, 62, 65, 66, 67, 68–69, 70, 71, 85
Narwhal, 135
Nashville, 75, 81, 85
Nassau, 131, 136, 145, 146
National Guard (U.S.), 19, 48
Nautilus, 69, 135
Naval Special Landing Force (Japan), 41
442nd Infantry Battalion (U.S.), 48
Nenohi, 90; capsizing of, 90
Netherlands, 4–5
Nevada, 131, 136

New Caledonia, 78
New Guinea, 107, 115, 153;
    Port Moresby, capture of,
    58, 59
New Mexico, 158
New Zealand, 57
Nimitz, Chester W., 27, 42–
    43, 61, 63–65, 67, 74–75,
    80, 85, 86–87, 89, 90, 110,
    113, 115, 130, 131, 155,
    168; forming North Pacific
    Force, 64, 75
Ninth Corps (U.S.), 9–10, 52
Nippon Maru, 159
Nissan Maru, 88; attack on,
    91
Nomura, Kichisabura, 8
Northern Area Force (Japan),
    167
Northern Landing Force
    (U.S.), 138, 147
North Pacific Force (U.S.),
    64, 75, 110, 154, 156
Northwestern, 84

Oite, 35
Omori, Rear Admiral, 85, 86
100th Infantry Battalion
    (U.S.), 48
Operation Landgrab, 130
Orange Plan (U.S.), 16
Oyodo, 137

Pacific Fleet (U.S.), 8, 10,
    15, 20, 38, 42, 43, 44, 54,
    55, 62, 65, 106, 115
P-38 aircraft, 94, 95, 97, 98,
    100, 107, 108, 114, 115,
    116, 134, 142, 149, 150,
    158
P-39 aircraft, 97
P-40 aircraft, 20, 81, 83, 92,
    108–109, 114, 116, 134,
    158

Panama Canal, 2, 6, 10, 14,
    16, 17, 45
Panay incident, 3
PBY patrol planes, 62, 66,
    68, 84, 94, 98, 99, 103,
    107, 126, 149, 150, 160
PC-487, 155
Peale Island, 35
Pearl Harbor, 10, 12, 15, 17,
    22, 24–27, 32, 43, 50, 53
Penguin, 30
Pennsylvania, 131, 144, 145,
    146, 148
Phelps, 148, 149
Philippines, 10, 12, 22, 25,
    45, 62; Japanese assault on,
    29
Poindexter, Joseph B., 25
Portland, 161
Port Moresby, 58, 59, 63
Provisional Battalion (U.S.),
    48, 138–139, 143, 147
Pruitt, 136
Puerto Rico, 9
Pye, W. S., 38–39, 42, 43,
    44; as commander of
    Pacific Fleet, 39; difference
    between Kimmel and, 42

Rabaul, 59
Rainbow Four (U.S.
    hemispheric defense plan),
    6
Raleigh, 105
Reid, 103
Richardson, James O., 19–20
Richmond, 109, 118, 119,
    121, 124, 125; attack on,
    121
RO-61, 103
Rockwell, Francis W., 113,
    130, 134, 135, 136, 144–
    145, 146, 148; Brown,
    conference with, 144;

Rockwell, Francis W. (*cont.*)
postponing landing on Attu
Island, 134

Rodgers, Bertram J., 120,
121, 122

Rome-Berlin-Tokyo alliance,
3, 19

Roosevelt, Franklin D., 2, 6,
7, 9, 11, 17, 19–20, 23,
78; agreements between
Churchill and, 57; giving
approval for arrest and
internment of Japanese, 53;
interest in navy, 11;
ordering removal of
Kimmel, 42; pressing for
evacuation of Japanese in
Hawaii, 47–48

Roosevelt, Theodore, 10, 14;
Treaty of Portsmouth
negotiations, 14

Russells Islands, 115

Russo-Japanese war, 14

Ryujo, 82, 83, 87, 89

S-27, 89

S-28, 109

S-30, 156

S-31, 105

S-34, 104

S-41, 155

Sakita Maru, 116

Salt Lake City, 118–126, 132;
attack on, 121, 122, 125;
dead in water, 125, 126

Sand Island, 68

San Francisco, 37, 106, 161

Sanko Maru, 116, 120

Santa Fe, 132

Sarana Bay, 129–131

Saratoga, 36, 37, 39, 43, 44,
64, 72, 86; attack on, 64

Second Battalion (U.S.), 139,
142

Second Marine Raider
Batallion (U.S.), 63

Second Mobile Force (Japan),
65, 82

Seventeenth Infantry First
Battalion (U.S.), 138, 139,
140, 143, 154

Seventeenth Infantry
Regimental Combat Team
(U.S.), 130, 150, 152

Seventh Division (U.S.), 113,
128, 130, 132, 144, 152

Seventh Reconaissance Troop
(U.S.), 139–140, 142, 147

Shannon, Harold, 63

Shasta, 145

Shemya Island, 106, 130,
141, 144

Sherrod, Robert, 151

Shimushu Island, 157–158

Shinano, 11

Shiranuhi, 90

Shokaku, 59, 65, 137

Short, Walter C., 10, 20–23,
25–26, 27, 46, 48; as
commander of Army
Hawaii Department, 20

Sicard, 135

Sixth Fleet (Japan), 38, 51

Smith, H. T., 95–96

Smith, Howland M., 113, 163

Solomon Islands, 58, 61, 107,
153

Soryu, 39, 71; attack on, 71

Southern Landing Force
(U.S.), 139, 141, 147

Spruance, Raymond, 64, 67,
69, 70

St. George Island, 97

St. Lawrence Island, 93

St. Louis, 75, 104

St. Paul Island, 97

Stalin, Joseph, 153

Stark, Admiral, 42

Stimson, Henry L., 7, 20
Suzuya, 137

Taiwan, 29
"Tales of Kiska" (Byron),
   165–166
Tama, 116, 119–120, 122–
   123, 159; attack on, 123
Tanga Island, 95, 96, 99,
   106; Buckner's plan for
   occupation of, 95
Tangier, 36–37, 43
Task Force Eight (U.S.), 75
Tatsuta, 34, 35, 39
TBF bombers, 67–68
Tenryu, 34, 35, 39
Theobald, Robert A., 75, 76,
   80–81, 84–85, 87, 89, 91,
   94, 95, 96, 97, 98, 99,
   101, 104; personality clash
   between Buckner and, 100;
   turning seagoing command
   over to Smith, 95
Third Battalion (U.S.), 139,
   141, 142, 143, 147
Thirteenth Naval District
   (U.S.), 74
Thirty-second Infantry (U.S.),
   130, 145–146, 152
Thirty-fifth Division (U.S.),
   113
343 Fighter Group (U.S.), 99,
   114
Time magazine, 151
Tōjō, Hideki, 77, 153; code
   of conduct to guide
   Imperial Japanese Army,
   writing, 153
Tone, 39, 137
Treaty of Portsmouth, 14
Triton, 90; 91
Tulagi, 59
Twelfth Area Fleet (Japan),
   167

Twenty-first Bombardment
   Squadron (U.S.), 97, 99

Umnak Island, 80, 81, 83,
   85, 95, 97
United States: Alaskan
   defenses, 73–76, 78, 80;
   American-Canadian
   Permanent Joint Board on
   Defense, 4, 5; Army Air
   Force, 18; arrest and
   internment of Japanese, 53;
   Attu Islands, knowledge of,
   128; celebrating reconquest
   of Aleutians, 167; decision
   to avoid war with Japan, 7;
   defense of Hawaii, 14–27;
   defense perimeter, 5; Good
   Neighbor Policy, 4; Great
   White Fleet, 10;
   hemispheric defense plan,
   6; Hepburn Board
   recommendations for
   improving defenses, 12–13,
   31; imprisonment of entire
   West Coast Japanese
   population, 52; Japanese
   occupation of Indochina,
   response to, 7; Joint Chiefs
   of Staff, 92–93, 96–97,
   101, 111, 115, 154, 168–
   169; Monroe Doctrine, 4;
   naval arms race, 11–12;
   naval officers studying in
   Japan, 11; Orange Plan, 16;
   Pacific Ocean, assuming
   responsibility for defense of
   entire, 57; preparing for
   war, 9–13; problems of
   command, 92–101; radar,
   development of, 21;
   Rainbow Four (hemispheric
   defense plan), 6; registering
   all enemy aliens, 52;

United States (*cont.*)
reinforcing their perimeter,
62–63; Roberts report on
Pearl Harbor, publication
of, 53; sanctions against
Japan, 22; War Department,
18, 23, 50, 74, 92, 93,
113; War Relocation
Authority, establishing, 53;
Washington Naval Treaty of
1921, 16; Washington
Naval Treaty of 1922, 12;
West Coast defense, 50–53,
75–76; Western Defense
Command, 10, 50, 93
Usugumo, 137

*Ventura bombers, 156

Wakaba, 116, 120
Wake Island, 3, 10, 12–13,
22, 23, 31–45, 62; Japanese
invasion of, 34, 41;
Kimmel's recommendations
for strong defensive
measures for, 31, 36;
location of, 31; renaming
of, 45; as site of Pan
American Airways, 31;
unconditional surrender by
Cunningham and Devereux
to Japanese, 44–45
Waldron, John C., 70
Warden, 107
Washington Naval Treaty of
1921, 16

Washington Naval Treaty of
1922, 12
Western Defense Command
(U.S.), 10, 50, 93
Western Perimeter, 28–45
Wichita, 157, 161
Wilkes Island, 34, 35;
Japanese landing on, 41
William B. Preston, 29
Willoughby, William H., 139
World War I, 11

Yamamoto, Isoroku, 11, 39,
54–58, 62, 64, 66, 72, 85,
87, 96, 135; death of, 135;
decision to carry on
invasion of Aleutians, 85;
threatening to resign, 56
Yamato, 11, 66
Yamazaki, Yasuyo, 129, 135,
137, 149–150; burning
secret documents, 137
Yayoi, 35
Yorktown, 59, 64, 67, 71–72;
attack on, 72
Yubari, 34, 39

Zeitlin, 141
Zero fighters, 40, 67, 68, 95,
96, 102
Zimmerman, Wayne L., 142,
149–150; Distinguished
Service Cross awarded to,
152
Zuiho, 87, 89, 137
Zuikaku, 59, 64, 87, 89, 137